Milady's Standard
Nail Technology
Exam Review

Jeryl Geary

Australia Canada Mexico Singapore Spain United Kingdom United States

Milady's Standard: Nail Technology
Jeryl Geary

For permission to use material from this text or product, submit a request online at http://www.thomsonrights.com.

Any additional questions about permissions can be submitted by e-mail to thomsonrights@thomson.com
Library of Congress Cataloging-in-Publication Data
ISBN 1-4180-1624-1
ISBN 978-1-4180-1624-1

NOTICE TO THE READER

Publisher does not warrant or guarantee any of the products described herein or perform any independent analysis in connection with any of the product information contained herein. Publisher does not assume, and expressly disclaims, any obligation to obtain and include information other than that provided to it by the manufacturer.

The reader is expressly warned to consider and adopt all safety precautions that might be indicated by the activities herein and to avoid all potential hazards. By following the instructions contained herein, the reader willingly assumes all risks in connection with such instructions.

The Publisher makes no representation or warranties of any kind, including but not limited to, the warranties of fitness for particular purpose or merchantability, nor are any such representations implied with respect to the material set forth herein, and the publisher takes no responsibility with respect to such material.The publisher shall not be liable for any special, consequential, or exemplary damages resulting, in whole or part, from the readers' use of, or reliance upon, this material.

Milady's Standard Nail Technology Exam Review

Foreword

This book of exam reviews contains questions similar to those that may be found on state licensing exams for nail technology. It employs the multiple-choice type question, which has been widely adopted and approved by the majority of state licensing boards.

Groups of questions have been arranged under major subject areas. To get the maximum advantage when using this book, it is advisable that the review of subject matter take place shortly after its classroom presentation.

This review book reflects advances in professional nail technology. It attempts to keep pace with, and insure a basic understanding of, sanitation, anatomy, physiology, and salon business applicable to the nail technician, client consultation guidelines, chemical safety in the nail salon, and basic manicuring and pedicuring procedures as well as some of the more advanced and creative aspects of the profession.

The book serves as an excellent guide for the student as well as for the experienced nail technician. It provides a reliable standard against which professionals can measure their knowledge, understanding, and abilities.

Furthermore, these reviews will help students and professionals alike to gain a more thorough understanding of the full scope of their work as they review practical performance skills and related theory. They will increase their ability to evaluate new products and procedures and to be better qualified professionals for dealing with the needs of their clients.

Part I: Chapter Review Tests

Directions: Carefully read each statement. Insert on the blank line after each statement the letter representing the word or phrase that correctly completes the statement.

CHAPTER 1: HISTORY AND OPPORTUNITIES

1. Define kosmetikos.
   a) skilled in the use of cosmetics
   b) cosmetologist
   c) aesthetician
   d) nail technician
   _____

2. Which ancient civilization first created kohl makeup?
   a) Greeks
   b) Egyptians
   c) Chinese
   d) Romans
   _____

3. Different hair colors represented different classes in Roman society. Which of the following statements is not true?
   a) Blonde indicated middle class.
   b) Black indicated lower class.
   c) Red was reserved for the nobility.
   d) Brown had a religious connotation.
   _____

4. Queen Nefertiti _____ her nails with henna to create a rich orange-red color.
   a) decorated
   b) polished
   c) stained
   d) airbrushed
   _____

5. Currently there is a shortage of _____ in the salon industry because the demand for professional nail services has quadrupled over the past 5 years.
   a) manicure equipment
   b) nail supplies
   c) nail technicians
   d) acrylic (methacrylate) nail manufacturers
   _____

6. Acrylic (methacrylate) nails are what type of service?
   a) natural looking nail service
   b) natural nail enhancement
   c) nail tip
   d) artificial nail enhancement
   _____

7. UV gel nails are what type of service?
   a) manicure
   b) pedicure
   c) fortifying
   d) artificial nail enhancement
   _____

8. What did Jeff Pink, founder of Orly International, create in 1974?
    a) French manicure   b) Juliet wrap
    c) acrylic nails   d) nail hardener   _____

9. How do you achieve rapid success in the nail care business?
    a) focus on your studies   b) attend workshops outside of school
    c) practice, practice, practice   d) all the above   _____

10. Charles Revson is so important to modern-day nail services because:
    a) he invented and marketed the first nail polish   b) he invented nail polish
    c) he perfected top coat   d) he was responsible for designing the first pair of nail nippers   _____

11. In 1999, what groundbreaking system did Creative Nail Design introduce to the professional beauty market?
    a) the first spa pedicure system   b) nail tips
    c) acrylic nail products   d) the curette   _____

12. We know that personal grooming and enhancement has been important since the dawn of history through archeological finds that include:
    a) mirrors, lip color, and combs   b) animal sinew, sharpened flints, bones and oyster shells fashioned into combs and hair ornaments
    c) rawhide hair decorations   d) tattoos for decoration   _____

13. Among many firsts, the Egyptians were the first civilization to:
    a) cultivate beauty in an extravagant fashion   b) extract essential oils
    c) use nail color   d) paint their lips   _____

14. The first known cosmetics factory was built by which famous beauty?
    a) Queen Cleopatra   b) Queen Nefertiti
    c) Gloria Swanson   d) Empress Eugenie   _____

15. In 1600 B.C., a tinted mixture of gum arabic, gelatin, beeswax, and egg whites was used by Chinese aristocrats to:

    a) create eye makeup in dazzling colors   b) color their nails crimson or ebony

    c) fortify their nails   d) soften their skin   _____

16. Egyptians used heavy amounts of kohl makeup to:

    a) alleviate eye inflammation   b) protect the eyes from glare

    c) beautify the eyes   d) all the above   _____

17. Nail technicians have many career choices, including:

    a) distributor sales consultant   b) editorial nail artist

    c) retail sales and management   d) all the above   _____

CHAPTER 2: LIFE SKILLS

1. The salon is a _____ by nature.
   - a) customer-service oriented business
   - b) place to exercise your creative talent
   - c) highly social atmosphere
   - d) all of the above

   _____

2. Game plan can best be defined as:
   - a) the conscious act of planning your life
   - b) always focusing on success
   - c) knowing what you will be doing 1 month from now
   - d) having goals that will further your career

   _____

3. When you have _____, staying on course for your entire career is much easier.
   - a) great life skills
   - b) good attitude
   - c) consistency in your work
   - d) good concentration

   _____

4. How should you greet your next client even if you have just worked 7 hours straight without a break?
   - a) by acting exhausted
   - b) with the best smile you can muster
   - c) with a handshake
   - d) with genuine enthusiasm

   _____

5. You should _____ any time studying for two hours at a stretch makes you feel overwhelmed.
   - a) take a two-hour break
   - b) study in shorter chunks of time
   - c) eat sugar and keep studying
   - d) condition yourself to study for longer periods of time.

   _____

6. What stimulates clear thinking and career planning?
   - a) competing in sports events
   - b) dancing and socializing
   - c) recreation and rest
   - d) all the above

   _____

7. Define "perfectionism."
   - a) unhealthy desire to always be perfect
   - b) ability to be perfect in certain things
   - c) paying attention to detail
   - d) appearing flawless

   _____

8. Having faith in your ability to reach your goals is called:
   a) being conceited
   b) having good self-esteem
   c) an affirmation
   d) being self-absorbed   _____

9. Which of the following describe(s) sensitivity?
   a) understanding
   b) empathy
   c) acceptance
   d) all the above   _____

10. How should you prioritize your tasks when practicing time management?
    a) treat all tasks equally
    b) make a chart
    c) easiest to hardest
    d) most to least important   _____

11. The most ideal place to study is:
    a) in a classroom where studying is the norm
    b) outdoors where the air is fresh and you can concentrate
    c) in a comfortable spot where you can lay down and feel relaxed
    d) in a quiet spot where you can study uninterrupted   _____

12. Staying on course with your career requires:
    a) a good education
    b) excellent social skills
    c) having stamina
    d) great life skills   _____

13. The salon requires strong _____ in order to always act in a professional manner.
    a) sense of humor
    b) allies
    c) self-discipline
    d) family support   _____

14. Listening attentively is:
    a) a trick
    b) tougher for men
    c) a natural talent
    d) a life skill   _____

15. A necessary _____ is seeing jobs through to completion.
    a) life skill
    b) natural characteristic
    c) task
    d) talent   _____

16. Guiding principles are:
    a) principles that guide your behavior
    b) meditative phrases
    c) a set of beliefs
    d) guidelines for negative behavior   _____

17. Respecting others is a:
    a) code of ethics   b) guiding principle
    c) life skill   d) rule of etiquette   _____

18. Which of the following is not one of the 10 guiding principles?
    a) having good   b) having all materials at
       self-esteem   the ready
    c) striving for excellence d) being consistent with
                                your work   _____

19. What is procrastination?
    a) not starting tasks until b) putting off until
       they are due   tomorrow what you
                                    can do today
    c) being lazy   d) delaying your success   _____

20. Every successful business follows what?
    a) a benefits manual   b) a sound business plan
    c) a monthly meeting   d) future plans
       plan   _____

21. What is the greatest benefit of setting goals?
    a) details your ambitions b) keeps you organized
    c) helps determine your   d) helps determine what
       immediate needs   you want out of life   _____

22. A long-term goal is which length of time?
    a) a week or longer   b) 6 months
    c) 5 years   d) 3 months   _____

23. Your mission statement should communicate:
    a) who you are; what you b) who you are; what you
       want out of life   want others to think
                                 about you
    c) who you are; what you d) who you are; how
       like   much money you want
                                 to earn   _____

24. Your personal mission statement should be read:
    a) every week   b) when you are stressed
    c) every day   d) three times a day   _____

25. Time management involves doing things in what order?
    a) least to most important b) most to least important
    c) morning, afternoon,   d) alphabetical order
       and evening activities   _____

26. What does ethics mean?
    - a) being faithful to your significant other
    - b) moral principles that you live and work by
    - c) never cheating on a test
    - d) being a kind person
    _____

27. Receptivity involves what?
    - a) hearing clearly
    - b) being a good listener
    - c) being open-minded
    - d) being empathetic
    _____

28. What is diplomacy?
    - a) being tactful
    - b) being political
    - c) being aggressive
    - d) being assertive, but tactful
    _____

29. Good _____ means communicating clearly and directly with others.
    - a) speaking skills
    - b) communication skills
    - c) people skills
    - d) diction
    _____

30. Define time management.
    - a) saving enough time to study
    - b) doing less things in more time
    - c) making efficient use of your time
    - d) doing more things in less time
    _____

CHAPTER 3: YOUR PROFESSIONAL IMAGE

1. Your personal image is important to your career because:
   - a) you belong to the trend business
   - b) it is part of looking professional
   - c) you are in the image business
   - d) dressing fashionably will build your clientele _____

2. Define personal hygiene.
   - a) daily maintenance of cleanliness through sanitary practices
   - b) thorough hand washing
   - c) wearing deodorant
   - d) wearing clean, stain-free clothing _____

3. What is a hygiene pack?
   - a) pouch of hygiene products that should be kept at home
   - b) pack you give to other stylists when they have bad breath or body odor
   - c) pack that is only used during beauty school
   - d) collection of personal hygiene products that you keep at your station or in your locker _____

4. If you have bad body odor, what are clients most likely to do or say?
   - a) hand you a breath mint
   - b) say nothing, but continue to have you do their nails
   - c) say nothing, but find another nail technician if the problem persists
   - d) tell you that you have offensive body odor and suggest that you do something about it _____

5. Your hygiene pack should include a:
   - a) toothbrush and toothpaste
   - b) mouthwash
   - c) hand sanitizer
   - d) all the above _____

6. What should you do if you smoke a cigarette before caring for a client?
   - a) brush your teeth and use mouthwash
   - b) wash hands
   - c) use perfume
   - d) brush your teeth, use mouthwash, and wash your hands _____

7. Which of the following best applies to wearing perfume in the workplace?
   a) Keep perfume usage to a minimum, if at all.
   b) Wear only the latest fragrances.
   c) Only dab it behind your ears.
   d) Apply it only once a day. _____

8. It is important for a nail technician to wear the latest hairstyle, haircolor, and makeup application because it:
   a) lets others know you do fashion forward services
   b) inspires clients and instills confidence in your work
   c) helps you bond with the stylists
   d) increases the amount of tips per service _____

9. In terms of hygiene, clothing should:
   a) be appropriate for your figure
   b) be modest
   c) look fresh and new
   d) be stain free and soil free _____

10. _____ is an important part of having a good physical presentation.
   a) Good posture
   b) A pleasing walk
   c) Eloquent movements
   d) A graceful stride _____

11. While doing nails, good posture includes:
   a) keeping legs and hips straight
   b) keeping head level with shoulders
   c) lifting upper body—do not slouch
   d) standing with your back straight _____

12. Repetitive motion syndrome that results in injury to the wrist is called:
   a) carpal tunnel syndrome
   b) myofascial spasm
   c) phlebitis
   d) endocarpal syndrome _____

13. Carpal tunnel syndrome can be partly avoided by:
   a) taking a 30-minute break between appointments
   b) using ergonomically designed implements
   c) gripping implements tightly
   d) keeping your elbows at least 60 degrees away from your body _____

14. When performing nail services, always:

    a) bend forward to get closer to clients

    b) remember that clients'comfort comes first

    c) avoid bending forward; ask clients to move their hands or legs closer to you

    d) make sure that your chair supports your upper back

    _____

15. What does ergonomics entail?

    a) sanitation practices

    b) OSHA regulations

    c) maximum comfort in the workplace

    d) designing the workplace for maximum comfort, safety, efficiency, and productivity of workers

    _____

16. Which of the following has a cumulative effect on the muscles and joints:

    a) using an airbrush system

    b) rigid posture

    c) applying nail tips

    d) stressful, repetitive motions

    _____

17. What does dress code mean?

    a) maintaining an edgy appearance

    b) salon rules regarding the correct manner of dress for that particular business

    c) wearing only black or white

    d) wearing a uniform

    _____

18. If you continue to perform unsafe tasks, what do you risk developing?

    a) inhibition of the circulatory system

    b) heart disease

    c) musculoskeletal disorders

    d) injury to the ulna

    _____

19. What is the guiding rule of makeup in the salon?

    a) maximize your best features

    b) only to be worn when you have time

    c) be edgy, even when the salon is not

    d) complement the colors of the salon

    _____

20. Define salon personality.

    a) personality of owner

    b) salon's overall image

    c) clients' preferences

    d) choice of music and decor

    _____

21. The best way to avoid developing a musculoskeletal disorder related to nail services is to:
    a) practice sound ergonomics
    b) never work more than 4 hours without a break
    c) do only three pedicures in an 8-hour day
    d) wear wrist guards while sleeping
    _____

22. Your clothing should always be clean, fresh, functional, and _____, whether or not you must abide by a salon dress code.
    a) cutting edge
    b) subdued
    c) embody the latest color trends
    d) stylish
    _____

23. What does MSD mean?
    a) muscular strain and development
    b) management of strains and disorders
    c) musculoskeletal disorders
    d) material safety data sheet
    _____

24. The risk of developing repetitive motion syndrome of the wrist can be minimized by:
    a) using only titanium implements
    b) keeping your wrist vertical with the table
    c) avoiding excessive bending of the wrist while using implements
    d) using your right and left hands equally
    _____

25. Doing this strengthens your hands:
    a) push-ups
    b) juggling
    c) pounding a rubber mat
    d) squeezing a hard rubber ball
    _____

26. Which of the following is an example of ergonomic equipment?
    a) pedicure stool on rollers
    b) halogen lamp
    c) manicure chair that can be raised and lowered
    d) vibrating pedicure chair
    _____

27. You can show off your figure and convey an image of self-confidence when you:
a) have a great personality
b) have good posture
c) give thought to your appearance
d) have a pleasant demeanor

_____

CHAPTER 4: COMMUNICATING FOR SUCCESS

1. You are in a better position to _____ when you clearly understand the motives and needs of others.
   - a) make the right decisions
   - b) do your job professionally and easily
   - c) lend a sympathetic ear
   - d) give good advice   _____

2. To be a successful beauty professional, you must have great:
   - a) personality traits
   - b) communication skills
   - c) mechanical skills
   - d) chemistry   _____

3. Before you can _____, you must have a firm understanding of yourself.
   - a) be attractive to the opposite sex
   - b) be a great nail artist
   - c) be certain of your career as a nail technician
   - d) understand others   _____

4. What must you do to successfully handle difficult clients?
   - a) Be aware of how you are feeling.
   - b) Pay close attention to what clients are saying.
   - c) Believe in yourself.
   - d) All the above.   _____

5. The golden rules of human relations teach you how to:
   - a) create a fan club
   - b) win people's hearts and support
   - c) be an effective social climber
   - d) treat people fairly and kindly   _____

6. The golden rules of human relations teach you to problem solve from your head and:
   - a) communicate from your heart
   - b) speak your mind
   - c) avoid problems with your mind
   - d) empathize with your soul   _____

7. When a tense situation arises, you should:
   - a) react slowly
   - b) avoid the situation
   - c) act proactively
   - d) remain calm   _____

8. When two people disagree on a certain subject, what should they do?
   a) debate until one concedes
   b) understand the other person's point of view
   c) stop talking
   d) be offended _____

9. The golden rules of human relations stress the importance of knowing the difference between being right and being:
   a) wrong
   b) diplomatic
   c) narrow-minded
   d) righteous _____

10. What does communication mean?
   a) effectively sharing information
   b) talking clearly and loudly
   c) projecting your voice
   d) speaking the same language _____

11. Nail technicians communicate through words, voice inflections, facial expressions, body language, and:
   a) the quality of their own nails
   b) a sense of caring
   c) visual tools
   d) finding common ground with clients _____

12. Which of the following is a classic nail design?
   a) French manicure
   b) pale nail polish colors
   c) creme nail polish
   d) foiling _____

13. A client consultation involves:
   a) learning about her lifestyle
   b) having an informal chat about her nails
   c) asking questions
   d) a structured fact-finding protocol _____

14. Repeating back what a client says, using different words, is called:
   a) proactive listening
   b) reflective listening
   c) intuitive listening
   d) active listening _____

15. A quality client consultation does not include discussing a client's:
   a) lifestyle
   b) commitment
   c) personal problems
   d) personal style _____

16. How should you handle a tardy client when you still have time to do her nails?
    a) Let her know you can still do her nails because you happen to have a break in your schedule.
    b) Permanently remove her from your books.
    c) Teach her a lesson by not taking her.
    d) Take her and say nothing. _____

17. When dealing with an unhappy client, what should you never do?
    a) Give her choices to rectify the problem.
    b) If you cannot immediately fix the problem, tell her why.
    c) Argue with her.
    d) Empathize with her feelings. _____

18. Your sole responsibility to your clients is to:
    a) be emotionally and professionally supportive
    b) take care of their beauty needs
    c) listen to their problems
    d) offer personal advice _____

19. Which of the following answer(s) describe(s) professional salon behavior?
    a) being honest and sensitive
    b) treating everyone with respect
    c) keeping your private life private
    d) all the above _____

20. When you disagree with a salon policy, what should you do?
    a) Discuss this issue with your coworkers.
    b) Bring it up at a staff meeting.
    c) Respect and follow that rule.
    d) Circulate a petition. _____

21. An employee evaluation involves a:
    a) meeting where you are either fired or hired as a permanent employee
    b) performance evaluation
    c) checklist of salon faults
    d) checklist of your faults _____

22. A client intake form is a:
    a) financial form
    b) questionnaire that includes contact info, past history of nail services, and so on
    c) quiz about nail services
    d) list of clients' previous nail technicians and whether or not they were happy with their services
    _____

23. The manager's job in a salon situation is to:
    a) help with personal problems
    b) make sure the salon runs smoothly
    c) mediate conflicts between coworkers
    d) all of the above
    _____

24. A(n) _____ cover health and lifestyle issues that could be contraindicative of having a nail service.
    a) consultation and intake form
    b) consultation and observing client's nails
    c) consultation and body language
    d) intake form and her body language
    _____

25. During a nail consultation, which tool(s) should you be using?
    a) drawing of nail shapes
    b) magazine clips
    c) personal portfolio
    d) all the above
    _____

CHAPTER 5: INFECTION CONTROL: PRINCIPLES AND PRACTICE

1. EPA stands for:
   a) Environmental Protection Agency
   b) Electrical Power Agency
   c) Etiology and Pest Association
   d) Environment Protection Association _____

2. How are bacteria classified?
   a) saprophytes and parasites
   b) pathogenic and nonpathogenic
   c) decomposing and fertilizing
   d) active and inactive _____

3. _____ are harmful and disease-producing pathogenic bacteria that invade plant or animal tissue.
   a) Saprophytes
   b) Cocci
   c) Parasites
   d) Spore-forming bacteria _____

4. Bacteria that live on dead and decaying matter are called:
   a) saprophytes
   b) cocci
   c) parasites
   d) spore-forming bacteria _____

5. How many cells make up a bacterium?
   a) two cells
   b) one cell
   c) three molecules
   d) pathogenic _____

6. _____ occurs when a bacterial cell divides into two new cells.
   a) Decomposing
   b) Fertilizing
   c) Mitosis
   d) Cell division _____

7. The most common kind of human bacteria are:
   a) staphylococci
   b) bacilli
   c) spirilla
   d) streptococci _____

8. What type of microscopic organisms are capable of infecting almost all plants, animals, and bacteria?
   a) infections
   b) fungus
   c) parasites
   d) virus _____

9. The pus-forming bacteria that grow in bunches or clusters are called:
   a) streptococci
   b) staphylococci
   c) bacilli
   d) pathogenic organisms _____

10. One example of a general infection is:
    a) a boil   b) a skin lesion
    c) a spherical spore   d) blood poisoning   _____

11. _____ gives us the ability to fight off or resist infections.
    a) Community resistance b) General infection
    c) Immunity   d) Contagious infection   _____

12. When you have immunity through inoculation or overcoming
a disease, it is called:
    a) human disease   b) natural immunity
       resistor
    c) acquired immunity   d) acquired immune
                      deficiency syndrome   _____

13. Acquired immune deficiency syndrome or AIDS is caused
by what virus?
    a) filterable bacteria   b) HIV
    c) HBV virus   d) filterable virus   _____

14. When you kill all living organisms on a surface, what is it
called?
    a) sanitation   b) sterilization
    c) removing bacteria   d) laundering   _____

15. When you kill most microbes on contaminated tools and
other nonliving surfaces, you are using a:
    a) disinfectant   b) styptic
    c) virucide   d) antiseptic   _____

16. Identify the correct answer that lists all three levels of
decontamination.
    a) sterilization,   b) disinfection,
       disinfection, sanitation   sanitation, laundering
    c) sterilization,   d) disinfection,
       disinfection,   sterilization, ultrasonic
       fumigation   cleansing   _____

17. You are _____ a surface when you significantly reduce
the number of pathogens by removing debris and using
warm, soapy water.
    a) sterilizing   b) fumigating
    c) sanitizing   d) disinfecting   _____

18. _____ include dirt, oils, and microbes.
    a) Contaminants   b) Spores
    c) Sanitizers   d) Pathogens   _____

19. When you eradicate pathogens and other substances from your implements, you are _____ or killing those pathogens.
    a) fumigating
    b) exterminating
    c) discouraging growth of bacteria
    d) sanitizing
    _____

20. HIV commonly infects individuals through:
    a) blood transfusions
    b) dirty hypodermic needles
    c) sexual contact with an infected person
    d) all the above
    _____

21. To properly disinfect your implements, they must be _____ for the prescribed amount of time.
    a) dipped
    b) washed
    c) completely immersed
    d) soaked
    _____

22. The Hazard Communication Rule does what?
    a) It requires chemical manufacturers and importers to assess the hazards associated with their products.
    b) Chemical manufacturers and importers no longer have to assess the hazards associated with their products.
    c) Licensed salon professionals must now assess the hazards associated with the products they are using.
    d) The salon owner is completely responsible for the hazards associated with any product they stock in their salon.
    _____

23. Ethyl alcohol must be no less than a _____ strength to be an effective disinfectant.
    a) 70%
    b) 90%
    c) 80%
    d) 50%
    _____

24. Sodium hypochlorite is the chemical name for this household staple:
    a) bathroom cleanser
    b) bleach
    c) phenolic disinfectant
    d) Lysol
    _____

25. QUATS is short for what?
    a) quaternary antiseptic compounds
    b) quaternary ammonium compounds
    c) quaternary ammonium treatments
    d) quaternary antiseptic solutions
    _____

26. Phenols may do what to certain rubber and plastic materials?
    a) soften and discolor   b) discolor and crack
    c) discolor and harden   d) soften and tear   _____

27. What information do MSDS (Material Safety Data Sheets) provide about products?
    a) combustion levels   b) associated hazards
    c) product content   d) all the above   _____

28. The _____ approves all disinfectants in each state.
    a) OSHA   b) EPA
    c) U.S. Department of   d) Chemists Society
    Labor   _____

29. Bacteria thrive in _____ environments.
    a) warm, moist, dirty   b) warm, dry, dirty
    c) cool, moist, dirty   d) cool, dry, dirty   _____

30. Bacteria can reach full growth in:
    a) 1 minute   b) 1 day
    c) 30 days   d) 30 minutes   _____

31. What is a local infection?
    a) confined to a single   b) confined to one organ
    area such as a pimple
    or infected cut
    c) confined to the face,   d) all the above
    hands, or feet   _____

32. What are bloodborne pathogens?
    a) disease-causing   b) disease-causing
    viruses   bacteria
    c) carried through the   d) all the above
    body in the blood or
    body fluids   _____

33. What must a disinfectant be to meet salon disinfection standards?
    a) pseudomonacidal,   b) pseudomonacidal,
    bactericidal,   bactericidal,
    fungicidal, and   fungicidal, and
    virucidal   pesticidal
    c) sterilizer, bactericidal, d) disinfectant,
    fungicidal, and   bactericidal,
    virucidal   fungicidal, and
                               pesticidal   _____

34. Which answer(s) describe a phenolic disinfectant?
    a) corrosive material   b) tuberculocidal
                                    disinfectant
    c) caustic poison   d) all the above   _____

35. A set of guidelines published by OSHA that require the
    employer and the employee to assume that all human blood
    and body fluids are infectious for bloodborne pathogens is
    called:
    a) Control of Infectious   b) AIDs manual
       Diseases
    c) Universal Precautions   d) Be Prepared Manual   _____

CHAPTER 6: GENERAL ANATOMY AND PHYSIOLOGY

1. Define anatomy.
   - a) functions and activities performed by the body's structures
   - b) minute structures of the body that cannot be seen with the naked eye
   - c) structures of the body that can be seen with the naked eye
   - d) the basic units of all living things

   _____

2. Identify the most important role that cells perform in the human body.
   - a) constructive metabolism
   - b) forming a protective covering on body surfaces
   - c) mitosis
   - d) carrying out all life processes

   _____

3. There are _____ of cells in the human body.
   - a) millions
   - b) trillions
   - c) quadrillions
   - d) quintillions

   _____

4. The composition of a cell does not include:
   - a) protoplasm
   - b) centrosome
   - c) catabolism
   - d) nucleus

   _____

5. Cell metabolism is composed of two phases:
   - a) anabolism and canabolism
   - b) anabolism and catabolism
   - c) cathartic and lethargic
   - d) libation and privation

   _____

6. How many types of tissues are found in the human body?
   - a) five
   - b) ten
   - c) hundreds
   - d) three

   _____

7. The connective tissue's primary role is to:
   - a) support, protect, and bind together other tissues of the body
   - b) support, protect, and bind together different types of keratin
   - c) protect against aging skin
   - d) aid in coordination

   _____

8. Identify the primary role(s) of nerve tissues:
   a) carry messages to and from the brain; control all body functions
   b) carry messages to and from the organs; control organ functions
   c) carry messages to and from the heart, kidneys, and lungs
   d) keep the heart beating

   _____

9. Identify the role(s) of muscle tissue in the human body:
   a) balances the body; allows you to move
   b) allows you to make skilled movements; allows you to sit upright
   c) contracts and moves various parts of the body
   d) causes eye tics

   _____

10. The _____ excrete(s) water and waste products.
    a) liver
    b) pancreas
    c) stomach
    d) kidneys

    _____

11. Which is not a system of the body?
    a) circulatory
    b) pancreatic
    c) endocrine
    d) all the above

    _____

12. What is the skeletal system?
    a) gives form to the human body
    b) made up of bones and movable and immovable joints
    c) protects internal organs
    d) serves as attachments for muscles

    _____

13. How many bones are there in the human skeletal system?
    a) 206
    b) 260
    c) 226
    d) 602

    _____

14. Identify three movable joints.
    a) elbows, knees, and hips
    b) pelvis, wrists, and ankles
    c) ulna, radius, and carpus
    d) elbows, knees, and fingers

    _____

15. Define osteology.
    a) bone disease
    b) study of ligaments
    c) study of bones
    d) study of the hardness of bones

    _____

16. Muscles are made of what?
    a) millions of tiny protein   b) millions of ligaments
       filaments
    c) millions of epithelial   d) tough, fibrous tissue
       cells   _____

17. What is the humerus?
    a) uppermost, largest   b) inner bone of the
       bone of the arm   forearm
    c) smaller bone on the   d) largest palm bone
       thumb side of forearm   _____

18. Define myology.
    a) study of the nature,   b) study of the nature,
       structure, and function   structure, function,
       of the bones   and diseases of the
                                       nerves
    c) study of the nature,   d) study of the nature,
       structure, function,   structure, function of
       and diseases of the   the human body
       muscles   _____

19. The study of the nervous system and its disorders is called:
    a) histology   b) neurology
    c) osteology   d) trichology   _____

20. The three main divisions of the nervous system are:
    a) cerebrospinal,   b) central, peripheral,
       peripheral, and   and metabolic
       autonomic
    c) spinal, peripheral, and   d) central, sensory, and
       automatic   motor   _____

21. Which part of the cell body receives messages from other
    neurons?
    a) axon   b) dendrite
    c) axon terminal   d) nucleus   _____

22. The nervous system's primary structural units are called:
    a) mixed nerves   b) afferents
    c) neurons   d) efferents   _____

23. The sensory and motor nerve fibers that go from the brain
    and spinal cord to all parts of the body make up the:
    a) peripheral system   b) autonomic nervous
                                       system
    c) parasympathetic   d) central nervous
       system   system   _____

24

24. What is the role of the adductors?
    a) draw the fingers together
    b) spread the fingers
    c) protect against rheumatoid arthritis
    d) move the fingers from side to side _____

25. The little finger side of the arm and the palm of the hand are supplied by the _____ nerve and its branches.
    a) digital
    b) radial
    c) median
    d) ulnar _____

26. Which parts of the heart are responsible for allowing the blood to flow in only one direction?
    a) atria
    b) ventricles
    c) valves
    d) arteries _____

27. The sticky, salty fluid that circulates throughout the circulatory system is called:
    a) white corpuscles
    b) blood
    c) plasma
    d) red corpuscles _____

28. What do red and white blood cells and blood platelets flow through?
    a) white corpuscles
    b) hemoglobin
    c) red corpuscles
    d) lymph _____

29. What percentage of water is found in plasma?
    a) 60 percent
    b) 70 percent
    c) 80 percent
    d) 90 percent _____

30. What process breaks down food so that it can be assimilated by the body?
    a) exhalation
    b) digestion
    c) evacuation
    d) contraction _____

31. Which organ is responsible for converting certain elements from the blood into new compounds?
    a) endocrines
    b) glands
    c) exocrines
    d) carotids _____

32. The _____ system is another name for the digestive system.
    a) excretory
    b) elimination
    c) integumentary
    d) gastrointestinal _____

33. What separates the chest from the abdominal region and controls breathing?
    - a) pericardium
    - b) chest cavity
    - c) rib cage
    - d) diaphragm

    _____

34. The basic unit of all living things is called a:
    - a) nucleus
    - b) cell
    - c) protoplasm
    - d) neuron

    _____

35. For cells to reproduce, what must be in place?
    - a) the right temperature
    - b) the ability to eliminate
    - c) adequate supplies of food, oxygen, and water
    - d) all the above

    _____

36. The role of cell metabolism is to:
    - a) produce more daughter cells
    - b) provide cell nourishment
    - c) enable cells to reproduce
    - d) keep the cells from turning into fat cells

    _____

37. What does catabolism do?
    - a) breaks down fat cells
    - b) breaks down proteins so that they can be absorbed by other cells
    - c) breaks down complex compounds within cells into smaller ones
    - d) builds large molecules from smaller ones

    _____

38. How do cells react to toxins?
    - a) cause cells to become bloated
    - b) do not have an effect on cells
    - c) increase metabolism within the cell
    - d) cause cells to become impaired or die

    _____

39. What is mitosis?
    - a) human reproduction
    - b) glandular reproduction
    - c) cell reproduction
    - d) saliva reproduction

    _____

40. Fascia, ligaments, fat, and tendons are _____ tissue.
    - a) connective
    - b) protective
    - c) integumentary
    - d) muscular

    _____

41. What components are found in liquid tissue?
    a) lymph and white corpuscles
    b) blood and lymph
    c) saliva and blood
    d) red corpuscles and bile _____

42. Lungs supply the blood with:
    a) hydrogen
    b) nitrous oxide
    c) carbon dioxide
    d) oxygen _____

43. What is the role of the digestive system?
    a) breaks down gases
    b) changes food into nutrients and wastes
    c) sorts out different kinds of waste
    d) keeps your system well fed _____

44. The heart, veins, arteries, and capillaries comprise which system?
    a) blood system
    b) not part of a system
    c) respiratory system
    d) circulatory system _____

45. The muscular system:
    a) allows the body to move
    b) allows the body to move internally and externally
    c) allows for skilled movements
    d) makes motor function possible _____

46. The body's hardest substance can be found in the:
    a) bones
    b) skull
    c) teeth
    d) pelvis _____

47. The human body has _____ muscles.
    a) over 1,000
    b) over 300
    c) over 600
    d) about 100 _____

48. All these pertain to the makeup of muscles except:
    a) origin
    b) epithelial
    c) belly
    d) insertion _____

49. What are striated muscles?
    a) attached to the bone and are voluntarily controlled
    b) involuntary heart muscles
    c) involuntary muscles found in internal organs
    d) all the above _____

50. The hand's two most important muscles are:
    a) abductors and adductors
    b) pronators and supinators
    c) pectoralis major and pectoralis minor
    d) flexors and extensors
    _____

51. Muscles can:
    a) stretch but not contract
    b) contract but not stretch
    c) stretch and contract
    d) none of the above
    _____

52. What are the functions of the latissimus dorsi?
    a) control the shoulder blade and swinging movements of the arm
    b) control the neck and swinging movements of the arm
    c) control the hips and swinging movements of the legs
    d) control the trapezius muscle and swinging movements of the arms
    _____

53. The _____ assists in breathing and raising the arm.
    a) diaphragm
    b) deltoid
    c) serratus anterior
    d) triceps
    _____

54. The sensory nerves:
    a) carry impulses from sense organs to the brain
    b) enable you to sense touch, cold, and heat
    c) enable you to experience sight, hearing, taste, smell, and pain
    d) all the above
    _____

55. What is the most important function of the lymph vascular system?
    a) aids in digestion
    b) carries waste and impurities away from the cells
    c) nourishes the cells
    d) protects against Hodgkin's disease
    _____

56. Which nerve and its branches supply the fingers?
    a) digital nerve
    b) radial nerve
    c) ulnar nerve
    d) median nerve
    _____

57. The pulmonary system and the _____ are responsible
for carrying blood throughout the body.
    a) recirculating system   b) systemic or general
                                 circulation system
    c) lymph system   d) hemoglobin   _____

58. What are the names of the two main arteries that supply
blood to the hand?
    a) major and minor   b) ulnar and radial
    c) red and blue   d) pulmonary and
                                   circulatory system   _____

59. The platelets:
    a) aid in digestion   b) aid in blood clotting
    c) prevent anemia   d) fight infections   _____

60. The _____ defends against invading microorganisms
and toxins.
    a) red corpuscle   b) lymph vascular system
    c) liver   d) pancreas   _____

CHAPTER 7: SKIN STRUCTURE AND GROWTH

1. Which of the following is the largest organ of the body?
   a) intestines   b) hair
   c) integumentary system   d) skin   _____

2. The _____ consists of the stratum spinosum, stratum lucidum, and stratum corneum.
   a) epidermis   b) subcutaneous
   c) dermis   d) hypodermis   _____

3. Blood vessels, nerves, sweat glands, and oil glands are found in which layer of the skin?
   a) dermis   b) epidermis
   c) subdermis   d) stratum corneum   _____

4. How is skin nourished?
   a) Oxygen and nutrients are carried through the bloodstream.   b) Proteins and fats are carried through the lymphatic system.
   c) Enzymes provide skin with nourishment.   d) Skin does not need nourishment.   _____

5. The dermis is also called:
   a) true skin   b) cutis
   c) corium   d) all the above   _____

6. The _____ has nerve endings but no blood vessels.
   a) dermis   b) hypodermis
   c) epidermis   d) papillary   _____

7. What is the primary purpose(s) of the hypodermis?
   a) contains fats for use as energy   b) acts as a protective cushion
   c) gives smoothness and contour to the body   d) all the above   _____

8. The two types of pigment found in the skin are:
   a) pheomelanin and eumelanin   b) red and yellow melanin
   c) brown and black melanin   d) island of melanin, lentigo   _____

9. The largest network of nerve endings in the hand is found in the:
   a) knuckles   b) fingertips
   c) palm   d) dorsal   _____

10. What are collagen and elastin?
   a) flexible ligaments that hold the skin together.
   b) flexible protein fibers found within the dermis.
   c) fibrous bands that anchor the skin to the subcutaneous layer
   d) cells that help protect the skin against UV rays

   _____

11. Define the function of collagen:
   a) helps skin regain its shape
   b) provides form and strength to the skin
   c) is more abundant in adults
   d) eliminates redness in the skin

   _____

12. Which of the following are lifestyle habits that cause premature aging of the skin?
   a) excessive alcohol consumption
   b) smoking
   c) overexposure to UV rays
   d) all the above

   _____

13. _____ duct glands extract materials from the blood to form new substances.
   a) Sudoriferous and sebaceous
   b) Sudoriferous and arrector pili
   c) Liver and pancreas
   d) Sudoriferous and lymph

   _____

14. The glands that eliminate up to two pints of liquid daily are called:
   a) sebaceous glands
   b) sudoriferous glands
   c) livers
   d) skin

   _____

15. Body temperature is regulated by this gland:
   a) circulatory
   b) integumentary
   c) sudoriferous
   d) endocrine

   _____

16. The #1 cause of skin aging is long-term exposure to:
   a) sun
   b) fluorescent lights
   c) makeup
   d) gravity

   _____

17. You should refer your clients to a dermatologist when:
   a) moles have changed color, size, or shape
   b) pigmented spots have irregular borders
   c) skin unexpectedly bleeds or will not heal quickly
   d) all the above

   _____

18. After swimming or water play, what should you do?
    a) nothing if you are wearing a broad-spectrum sunscreen
    b) apply just a little sunscreen
    c) avoid applying sunscreen unless your sunscreen is not water resistant.
    d) reapply recommended amount of sunscreen _____

19. Which of the following professionals is qualified to diagnose a skin disorder?
    a) aesthetician
    b) nurse practitioner
    c) physician
    d) pharmacist _____

20. A bulla is a(n):
    a) large blister containing watery fluid
    b) round solid lump
    c) inflamed, pus-filled pimple
    d) flat, discolored spot _____

21. A wheal is a(n):
    a) abnormal mass caused by excessive multiplication of cells
    b) closed, fluid-filled mass below the surface of the skin
    c) itchy, swollen lesion that lasts a few hours
    d) small blister or sac containing clear fluid _____

22. What are flaky, dry, or oily scales such as dandruff called?
    a) ulcers
    b) scales
    c) fissures
    d) cicatrix _____

23. Define excoriation.
    a) deep lesion
    b) superficial scratch
    c) gash
    d) rash _____

24. Define comedo.
    a) whitehead
    b) blackhead
    c) hair follicle filled with keratin and sebum
    d) milia _____

25. What is asteatosis?
    a) halitosis
    b) seborrheic dermatitis
    c) rosacea
    d) lack of sebum due to old age _____

26. Miliaria rubra is the medical name for:
    a) inability to sweat   b) offensive body odor
    c) prickly heat   d) psoriasis   _____

27. Dermatitis is a(n):
    a) contagious skin rash   b) inflammation of the
                                      skin caused by an
                                      allergic reaction or
                                      skin irritant
    c) condition   d) form of eczema
       characterized by
       silver-white scales   _____

28. Which type of dermatitis poses the greatest concern for nail
    technicians?
    a) formaldehyde   b) mite-related dermatitis
       dermatitis
    c) general dermatitis   d) contact dermatitis   _____

29. How can clients develop contact dermatitis to a nail
    ingredient?
    a) being exposed to   b) being exposed to a
       fumes during acrylic   sensitizing nail product
       nail services   over a long period of
                                      time
    c) systemic reaction   d) nail ingredients are
       unrelated to exposure   natural sensitizers   _____

30. Nail technicians are most likely to develop contact dermatitis
    in which area(s)?
    a) between thumb and   b) palms
       index finger
    c) back of forearm   d) all the above   _____

31. Clients can eventually develop contact dermatitis to nail
    products when nail technicians:
    a) do not leave a 1/16"   b) apply a dry product
       free margin between   ratio-mix to the nail
       the product and skin
    c) apply an overly thin   d) overcure their UV gel
       coat of gel product   nail enhancements   _____

32. Oversize brushes should not be used to apply liquid-and-powder nail enhancements because this
    a) wastes product
    b) risks product contamination
    c) causes monomer or UV gel to touch the client's skin during application
    d) yields poor results
    _____

33. To ensure that your UV bulbs are adequately curing gel nail enhancements, you should:
    a) replace bulbs at least three times per year
    b) clean surfaces of bulbs on a daily basis
    c) use the lamp designed for your system
    d) all the above
    _____

34. The best way to know when your UV bulbs need to be changed is:
    a) to note any color changes
    b) when they start blinking
    c) the length of time they have been in use
    d) when they do not emit heat
    _____

35. What do bleach, strong cleaning agents, quats, solvents, and acetone have in common?
    a) too caustic for salon use
    b) potential skin irritants
    c) sanitizing agents
    d) diluted products
    _____

36. Nail technicians can avoid developing contact dermatitis by:
    a) wiping their table down after each client
    b) practicing meticulous sanitary practices
    c) wearing gloves when using acetone to remove nail polish
    d) wiping down products on a daily basis
    _____

37. What is a keratoma?
    a) bruise
    b) welt
    c) type of skin cancer
    d) callus
    _____

38. What does vitiligo look like?
    a) multihued warts
    b) blackening of the skin
    c) dark and light spots
    d) milky-white spots
    _____

39. What is the role of an antioxidant?
a) quenches free radical   b) works against natural
   activity   skin function
c) aids free radicals   d) contributes to DNA
                              damage within skin
                              cells   _____

40. Which of the following are three potent antioxidants?
a) K, S, and foxglove   b) A, C, E
c) B1, D3, and St. John's d) C, E, and F
   Wort   _____

41. Healthy skin should contain between _____ of water.
a) 85 and 90 percent   b) 45 and 55 percent
c) 50 and 70 percent   d) 75 and 77 percent   _____

42. When cells become dehydrated, what happens to them?
a) Skin becomes   b) They become
   weathered looking.   stronger.
c) They make more   d) They cannot function
   collagen.   properly.   _____

43. Even mild dehydration can cause:
a) rapid aging   b) daytime fatigue
c) memory loss   d) all the above   _____

44. You can lessen hunger without consuming calories by:
a) putting it out of your b) smelling the food you
   mind   crave
c) drinking a glass of   d) speeding up your
   water   metabolism   _____

CHAPTER 8: NAIL STRUCTURE AND GROWTH

1. What does natural nail mean?
   - a) free of nail polish
   - b) free of artificial enhancements
   - c) muted nail color
   - d) free of chemicals _____

2. A dehydrated nail:
   - a) is weak
   - b) is brittle
   - c) has a yellow tinge
   - d) cannot grow past the free edge _____

3. How can you improve the water content of dehydrated nails?
   - a) Have clients drink 8 glasses of water a day.
   - b) Have clients use hand cream every night.
   - c) Use a cuticle cream every morning.
   - d) Treat the nail plate with an oil-based nail conditioner and keep the nails polished. _____

4. Nails are primarily made of what?
   - a) melanin
   - b) densely compacted keratin
   - c) several different proteins
   - d) calcium _____

5. A healthy nail should contain _____ water.
   - a) 14 percent
   - b) 10 percent
   - c) 30 to 50 percent
   - d) 15 to 25 percent _____

6. What is the purpose of the epithelium bed?
   - a) creates deep folds of skin around nail plate
   - b) anchors the nail plate to the nail bed
   - c) anchors nail bed to the underlying bone
   - d) provides the underlying support for the nail plate _____

7. The _____ is the whitish half-moon shape at the base of the nail.
   - a) cuticle
   - b) eponychium
   - c) lunula
   - d) hyponychium _____

8. What forms the nail plate?
   - a) hyponychium
   - b) epithelial tissue
   - c) keratin
   - d) matrix cells _____

9. Poor nail growth can be caused by what?
   a) poor general health   b) injury to the matrix
   c) nail disorder or   d) all the above
      disease   _____

10. The nail plate consists of approximately _____ layers.
    a) 10   b) 100
    c) 500   d) 1,000   _____

11. The matrix is vital to the nail plate because:
    a) it prevents fungus from   b) it is where nail growth
       infesting the nail bed   begins
    c) it is the most active   d) nail growth would be
       part of the skin   sluggish without it   _____

12. The primary purpose of the cuticle is to:
    a) do nothing   b) help shape the nail
    c) hold the nail in place   d) protect against injury
                                    and infection   _____

13. The fastest nail growth is experienced by:
    a) men   b) women
    c) children   d) young adults   _____

14. Which season is credited for fastest nail growth?
    a) summer   b) spring
    c) winter   d) fall   _____

15. What influences the thickness, width, and curvature of the
    nail?
    a) length, width, and   b) length, width, and
       curvature of the matrix   curvature of the nail
                                    bed
    c) length, width, and   d) thickness, width, and
       curvature of the nail   curvature of the matrix
       folds   _____

16. The _____ nail grows the fastest.
    a) middle finger   b) thumb
    c) index   d) all nails grow the same   _____

17. Which parts make up the cuticular system?
    a) cuticle and   b) hyponychium and nail
       eponychium   bed
    c) specialized ligaments   d) all the above
       and nail folds   _____

18. It takes approximately _____ for the nail to grow from the base to the free edge.

    a) 4 to 6 months   b) 1 month

    c) 9 months   d) 1 year   _____

19. How long does it take for a toenail to grow from the base of the nail bed to the free edge?

    a) 1 year   b) 3 months

    c) 9 months   d) 6 months   _____

20. A highly curved nail is caused by what?

    a) flat nail bed   b) injury

    c) highly curved free   d) highly curved matrix
       edge   _____

21. The average adult fingernail grows _____ in 1 month.

    a) 1/10 inch   b) 1/4 inch

    c) 1/8 inch   d) 1/3 inch   _____

22. Nail growth is affected by:

    a) nutrition   b) exercise

    c) general health   d) all the above   _____

23. How does an adequate water content affect nails?

    a) toughens nails   b) makes nails more
                          flexible

    c) makes nails less   d) allows polish to remain
       flexible   true to color   _____

24. What is the purpose of nail grooves or tracks?

    a) Nails grow along these b) They signal poor
       tracks.   health.

    c) They do not exist.   d) They anchor the nail.   _____

CHAPTER 9: NAIL DISEASES AND DISORDERS

1. When skin is split at the base of the nail, what is it called?
   a) melanonychia
   b) hangnail
   c) furrow
   d) beau's break
   _____

2. A trumpet or pincer nail is a(n):
   a) scarring of the distal nail fold
   b) horizontal nail depression
   c) extremely thin and weak nail
   d) highly exaggerated nail curvature
   _____

3. What does nail psoriasis do to the nails?
   a) pits the nails
   b) causes onychorrhexis
   c) causes onychocryptosis
   d) causes onychophagy
   _____

4. Leukonychia spots are:
   a) a potentially fatal form of cancer
   b) a direct result of contact dermatitis
   c) white spots not related to health
   d) caused by calcium deficiency
   _____

5. Describe a bruised nail.
   a) White spots appear on nail plate.
   b) Purplish blood clot forms under the nail.
   c) Nail bed goes from blue to green.
   d) Nail has a bruised appearance for three days or less.
   _____

6. Nail discoloration can be caused by an external source or:
   a) internal problem
   b) too much beta carotene
   c) injury to the matrix
   d) poor lifestyle choices
   _____

7. Define onychocryptosis.
   a) a plicatured nail
   b) dark ridges
   c) infected ingrown nail
   d) ingrown nail
   _____

8. The pressure of an ingrown nail can be relieved by doing what?
   a) filing the nail corners square
   b) cutting away the sides of the nail
   c) gently curving the corners of the nail
   d) cutting the nail very short
   _____

9. When filing eggshell nails, what grit should you use?
   a) 240 grit or higher   b) 80 grit
   c) 100 grit   d) should not file at all   _____

10. What causes split or brittle nails?
    a) injury to the matrix   b) excessive use of
                                    cuticle removers
    c) aggressive filing   d) all the above
       techniques   _____

11. What does onychophagy cause?
    a) incurable fungus   b) scarring of the skin
                                    surrounding the nail
                                    plate
    c) onychocryptosis   d) melanoma   _____

12. Which of the following cause(s) beau's lines?
    a) pneumonia   b) adverse drug reaction
    c) heart failure   d) all the above   _____

13. What is onychia?
    a) green spot between   b) eggshell nails
       the natural nail and the
       nail enhancement
    c) inflammation around   d) abnormal damage to
       the matrix   the eponychium   _____

14. What causes onychia?
    a) improperly disinfected   b) waiting too long
       nail implements   between nail
                                    appointments
    c) nail polish remover   d) double-dipping a nail
                                    brush during a nail
                                    service   _____

15. Define fungi.
    a) parasites that cause   b) vegetable parasites
       bad foot odor   that can infect the
                                    hands and feet
    c) green parasites   d) parasites that lead to
                                    bacterial infections   _____

16. The discoloration that sometimes develops between the nail
    plate and the nail enhancement is caused by:
    a) mold   b) fungus
    c) bacteria   d) dirt   _____

17. An advanced bacterial infection between the nail plate and an artificial nail enhancement is _____ in color.
   a) yellow green
   b) brown
   c) orange
   d) brown black _____

18. How should you treat a client's fungus infection?
   a) Scrub the nail, soak in quats.
   b) Spray with a fungicide solution.
   c) Apply an antifungal cream.
   d) Refer to a physician. _____

19. Define onychomycosis.
   a) mold infection of the natural nail plate
   b) bacterial infection of the natural nail plate
   c) fungal infection of the natural nail plate
   d) none of the above _____

20. Nail psoriasis causes:
   a) nail roughness, random pits
   b) ragged free edge, evenly spaced rows of pits
   c) yellow and red spots under the nail plate
   d) all the above _____

21. What is the medical name for a foot fungus?
   a) tinea digitata
   b) pedius fungi
   c) tinea pedis
   d) tinea digiti _____

22. Ridges that run lengthwise on the nail plate can be caused by:
   a) leukemia
   b) frostbite
   c) overheating
   d) dehydration _____

23. Paronychia is more prevalent on the:
   a) toenails
   b) fingernails
   c) big toes
   d) thumbs _____

24. How should you treat nails that are brittle, are deeply split, and have vertical ridges?
   a) Fill split with fast-drying glue.
   b) Treat only if nail is not split down to the nail bed.
   c) Apply ridge filler.
   d) Buff away ridges, avoiding the split area. _____

25. Describe foot fungus.
    a) itchy red rash between   b) flaking
       the toes
    c) small blisters   d) all the above   _____

26. Define pyogenic granuloma.
    a) a serious condition   b) severe infection
       that contributes to   characterized by a
       several types of   lump of red tissue
       cancer, especially   growing up from the
       melanoma   nail bed to the nail
                                     plate
    c) mild infection   d) a parasitic condition
       characterized by a   that begins as a mild
       lump of pink tissue   fungal infection, and
       growing up from the   grows worse over time
       nail bed to the nail
       plate   _____

27. What are the attributes of a healthy nail?
    a) firm, inflexible, shiny,   b) flexible, shiny, thick,
       and slightly pink or   and slightly pink or
       yellow.   yellow
    c) firm, flexible, shiny,   d) firm, inflexible, thick,
       and slightly pink or   and slightly pink or
       yellow   yellow   _____

28. The _____ spread more germs that any other parts
    of the body.
    a) mouth and nose   b) hands and lips
    c) feet and nose   d) hands and feet   _____

29. Why is carefully examining your client's hands or feet prior
    to performing a service so important?
    a) your safety   b) your client's safety
    c) your safety, your   d) safety of those around
       client's safety, and the   you
       safety of those around
       you   _____

30. _____ is the most common bacterial nail infection.
    a) Pseudomonas   b) Pseudomonas
       aerobica   aeruginosa
    c) Pseudomonas   d) Pseudomonas
       botanica   prolifica   _____

31. While services are being performed, fungi and bacteria can be spread by:
    a) sneezing
    b) improper sanitation and disinfection practices
    c) unsanitary implements
    d) not using antibacterial soap when washing hands _____

32. You should decline to do a nail service any time:
    a) there is inflamed or infected skin
    b) there is broken skin or swelling
    c) a condition is present that may be contagious
    d) all the above _____

33. It is safe to perform nail services when this condition is present:
    a) onychosis
    b) onychophagy
    c) onychia
    d) paronychia _____

34. Cutting off living tissue during a manicure causes _____ to develop.
    a) hangnails
    b) furrows
    c) eggshell nails
    d) white spots _____

35. Tinea unguium is more commonly known by this name:
    a) scalp ringworm
    b) athlete's foot
    c) honeycomb ringworm
    d) nail ringworm _____

36. Onycholysis is caused by:
    a) physical injury
    b) allergic reaction of the nail bed
    c) health disorder
    d) all the above _____

37. What does onycholysis cause the nail to do?
    a) break off at the free edge
    b) fall off
    c) lift away from the nail bed without shedding
    d) discolor and crumble _____

CHAPTER 10: BASICS OF CHEMISTRY

1. Solid matter:
   a) has volume but not shape
   b) has shape and form
   c) lacks shape and volume
   d) has only volume
   _____

2. Matter exists in which forms?
   a) minerals and water
   b) solid, liquid, and gas
   c) water and oxygen
   d) nitrous oxide and gas
   _____

3. All matter is composed of:
   a) atoms
   b) carbon
   c) compounds
   d) hydrogen
   _____

4. Define element.
   a) solid
   b) simplest form of matter
   c) compound
   d) unique molecules
   _____

5. Define organic chemistry.
   a) study of nonchemical substances
   b) study of substances containing vegetable matter
   c) study of pesticide-free foods
   d) study of substances containing carbon
   _____

6. What is carbon?
   a) metallic element found in all living things
   b) nonmetallic element found in all living things
   c) naturally occurring element
   d) a form of energy
   _____

7. Define inorganic substances.
   a) substances like gas, oil, and coal
   b) substances that have never been alive
   c) all minerals
   d) water, air, and metals
   _____

8. How many naturally occurring elements are there in the universe?
   a) 112
   b) 93
   c) 100
   d) 90
   _____

9. Define atom.
   a) particles from which all matter is composed
   b) particles from which most matter is composed
   c) particles from which natural matter is composed
   d) particles from which inorganic matter is composed _____

10. Define physical property.
   a) color, odor, weight, and density
   b) characteristics determined without a chemical reaction
   c) chemical change
   d) changing form without forming a new substance _____

11. What are elemental molecules?
   a) two or more atoms of the same element that have been united physically
   b) aluminum foil
   c) two or more atoms of different elements that are united chemically
   d) substances made up of elements that have been combined physically, rather than chemically (e.g., concrete). _____

12. Identify one or more physical mixtures.
   a) concrete
   b) oxygen
   c) cornbread
   d) all the above _____

13. A physical mixture that contains two or more different substances is called:
   a) a solution
   b) a suspension
   c) an emulsion
   d) all the above _____

14. Define solute.
   a) certain miscible liquids
   b) a substance within a solution
   c) solvent
   d) solution _____

15. What is a suspension?
    a) solid particles distributed throughout a liquid medium that tend to separate over time
    b) surfactant
    c) moisture of two or more immiscible substances united with the aid of a binder or emulsifier
    d) immiscible liquid

    _____

16. Define solution.
    a) solute
    b) blended mixture of two or more liquids or solids dissolved in a liquid
    c) two pure substances blended together
    d) surfactant

    _____

17. Describe the head of a surfactant.
    a) hydrophilic or water loving and dissolves in water
    b) lipophilic or oil loving and dissolves in oil
    c) neither water loving nor oil loving
    d) dissolves in both water and oil to form an emulsion

    _____

18. Water-in-oil emulsions are:
    a) ointments
    b) oil droplets that are suspended in a water base
    c) surfactants
    d) water droplets that are suspended in an oil base

    _____

19. Oil-in-water emulsions have:
    a) a much greater amount of oil
    b) a much greater amount of water
    c) slightly more water than oil
    d) slightly more oil than water

    _____

20. Which of the following is not a powder?
    a) physical mixture of two or more finely ground solids, including minerals
    b) mixture of micronized talc and titanium dioxide
    c) pulverized wheat
    d) mixture of micronized talc and zinc oxide

    _____

21. Define glycerine.
    a) used as a solvent and moisturizer
    b) colorless liquid with a pungent odor
    c) used in place of ammonia to raise the pH
    d) volatile organic compound
    _____

22. Which of the following most accurately describe formaldehyde (formalin)?
    a) preservative
    b) toxic to inhale and cancer causing
    c) strong irritant
    d) all the above
    _____

23. Which of the following is the most complete definition of an ion?
    a) an atom or molecule that carries a negative electrical charge
    b) an atom or molecule that carries an electrical charge
    c) an ion with a positive electrical charge
    d) a cation under certain circumstances
    _____

24. Water molecules naturally ionize into _____ and _____.
    a) Hydrogen ions and anion ions.
    b) Water molecules do not ionize.
    c) Hydrogen ions and hydroxide ions.
    d) Hydrogen ions and cation ions.
    _____

25. Which ions are measured by the pH scale?
    a) water molecules that have naturally ionized into hydrogen ions and some into hydroxide ions
    b) only water molecules that have ionized into hydroxide ions
    c) water molecules that have ionized into cation and anion ions
    d) only water molecules that have ionized into hydrogen ions
    _____

26. What does the pH scale measure?
    a) the acidity of a liquid
    b) the alkalinity of a liquid
    c) both the acidic and alkaline quality of a substance
    d) the degree of acidity or alkalinity of aqueous solutions
    _____

27. The pH scale ranges from:
    a) 0 to 15
    b) 0 to 14
    c) 0 to 12
    d) 0 to 10
    _____

28. What does 7 represent on the pH scale?
    a) acidic pH   b) neutral pH
    c) alkaline pH   d) no pH   _____

29. How can matter be changed?
    a) physically   b) chemically
    c) physically and   d) cannot be changed
       chemically   _____

30. In which form(s) does matter exist?
    a) elements   b) compounds
    c) mixtures   d) all the above   _____

31. Quickly evaporating solutions are:
    a) weighty   b) made up of isopropyl
                             alcohol
    c) volatile   d) resolute   _____

32. Water, air, metals, and minerals are:
    a) elements   b) inorganic substances
    c) organic substances d) compounds   _____

33. Which of the following best describes matter?
    a) occupies space   b) has physical and
                             chemical properties
    c) exists as either a solid, d) all the above
       liquid, or gas   _____

34. What are carbon, oxygen, nitrogen. silver, and sulfur?
    a) elements   b) molecular substances
    c) compounds   d) all the above   _____

35. A pure substance:
    a) only has organic   b) is matter with a fixed
       additives   chemical composition
                             (one of a kind
                             matter) and constant
                             properties.
    c) is unadulterated   d) has a fixed chemical
                             composition   _____

CHAPTER 11: NAIL PRODUCT CHEMISTRY SIMPLIFIED

1. In order to accurately troubleshoot and solve common service breakdowns, you must have at least some basic knowledge of what?
   a) technical skills
   b) chemistry of your products
   c) ins-and-outs of a particular nail enhancement product
   d) experience
   _____

2. Are all odorless monomers vapor free?
   a) no
   b) yes
   c) depends on the brand
   d) only if the dappen dish is not designed properly
   _____

3. All the following are types of nail primer except:
   a) non-acid
   b) acid-free
   c) acid-base
   d) oil-based
   _____

4. What is the role of acetone in nail services?
   a) corrosive
   b) solvent
   c) adhesive
   d) solute
   _____

5. Define corrosive.
   a) material that can damage skin on contact
   b) acid-free primer with a neutral pH
   c) strong nail adhesive that causes two surfaces to stick together
   d) rust
   _____

6. What causes two surfaces to stick together?
   a) cross-linkers
   b) solutes
   c) adhesives
   d) solvents
   _____

7. What can you do to help avoid nail infections and lifting?
   a) scrubbing the hands and nails
   b) applying lots of primer
   c) roughing up the nail
   d) overfiling the natural nail
   _____

8. A _____ monomers can link together in less than 1 second.
   a) billion
   b) million
   c) trillion
   d) quadrillion
   _____

9. What is a common reason for enhancement breakdown?
   a) removing natural oils from the nail plate
   b) applying corrosives to the nail
   c) removing surface moisture
   d) not completely removing oil and moisture from the nail plate

   _____

10. Define monomer.
    a) individual molecules that join together to make a polymer chain
    b) a chain nearly as large as a polymer chain
    c) clusters of molecules that join to make a polymer chain
    d) double chains of polymers

    _____

11. Good adhesion begins with:
    a) corrosion
    b) clean, dry nails
    c) antibacterial spray
    d) buffed surface

    _____

12. Monomers are cross linkers when they join different _____ together.
    a) initiators
    b) polymer chains
    c) histamines
    d) adhesives

    _____

13. What are the maintenance rules for UV bulbs?
    a) clean daily, replace two to three times a year
    b) clean weekly, replace once a month
    c) clean monthly, replace every three months
    d) maintain every quarter

    _____

14. What is the most common (and avoidable) skin condition suffered by nail technicians?
    a) psoriasis
    b) tinea pedis
    c) pachyonychia
    d) contact dermatitis

    _____

15. How do nail polishes, top coats, and base coats harden?
    a) polymerization
    b) different monomers
    c) through a chemical process
    d) they are evaporation coatings

    _____

16. What causes skin allergies, also called contact dermatitis, to monomers?
    a) occasional contact
    b) long-term exposure
    c) breathing too many fumes
    d) failure to sanitize properly

    _____

17. Why is it important to clean UV bulbs daily and replace them two to three times a year unless specified otherwise by the manufacturer?
    a) Unsatisfactory results alienate clients.
    b) Improperly cured nails may not last as expected.
    c) Improperly cured nails may eventually cause an allergic reaction.
    d) All the above.
    _____

18. The best thing clients can do for their natural nails is to:
    a) apply acrylic (methacrylate) artificial enhancements
    b) apply gel nails
    c) enlist the services of a skilled and educated nail technician
    d) apply nail strengtheners
    _____

19. Which body system responds when the skin is irritated by an outside substance?
    a) immune
    b) muscular
    c) circulatory
    d) respiratory
    _____

20. How is toxicity determined?
    a) skin condition
    b) time of year
    c) overexposure
    d) general health
    _____

21. When the skin is irritated, how does the immune system respond?
    a) It calls up an army of white cells.
    b) It summons a flood of red cells to the area.
    c) It coordinates the release of histamines.
    d) All the above.
    _____

22. It is important for nail technicians to have a basic understanding of chemistry because:
    a) they handle dangerous chemicals
    b) they could create explosive or corrosive situations
    c) they must constantly mix chemicals as part of their services
    d) almost everything they do depends on chemistry
    _____

23. The protein that makes up nails is mostly made from chemical(s) called:
    a) amino acids
    b) sulfur
    c) copper
    d) silver
    _____

24. Define molecule.
    a) physical change
    b) chemical in its simplest form
    c) vapor
    d) amino acid
    _____

25. What are corrosive nail primers called?
    a) acid primers
    b) acid-free primers
    c) non-acid primers
    d) alkaline primers
    _____

26. Corrosive acid-based primers can potentially:
    a) burn the nail bed
    b) damage the nail plate
    c) thin the nail plate
    d) all the above
    _____

27. Which of the following aid(s) in good adhesion?
    a) proper technique
    b) high-quality products
    c) washing the hands and scrubbing the nail plate
    d) all of the above
    _____

28. With acid-free primers and non-acid primers:
    a) there are no known allergic reactions
    b) skin contact must be avoided
    c) acrylic nails are much easier to apply
    d) nails degrade easily
    _____

29. What is the most common result of improper nail preparation?
    a) nail lifting
    b) product breakdown
    c) allergic reactions
    d) yellowing
    _____

30. All nail enhancements form:
    a) vapors
    b) noticeable odors
    c) infections
    d) none of the above
    _____

31. Nail products that improve artificial nail adhesion are called:
    a) base coat
    b) primers
    c) sticky base coat
    d) monomers
    _____

32. Primers should be used:
    a) rarely
    b) sparingly
    c) generously
    d) every other time you perform a rebase service.
    _____

33. You should always _____ any time you are having lifting problems.
    a) apply a second coat of primer
    b) review your application techniques and products
    c) make sure the client is not being careless at home
    d) decide that her nails are not a good candidate for artificial nail enhancements   _____

34. You should always dehydrate one hand at a time because:
    a) dust quickly settles on the nails
    b) bacteria quickly recolonize on natural nails
    c) oil and moisture return to the natural nail within 30 minutes
    d) dehydration can damage the nail plate   _____

35. Overfiling the nail plate creates a _____ for artificial nail enhancements.
    a) weaker foundation
    b) stronger foundation
    c) more natural flexibility
    d) more natural appearance   _____

36. Overfiling (thinning) the nail plate causes what?
    a) free-edge product separations and breaking
    b) allergic reactions and infections under the nail plate
    c) painful friction burns and nail chipping
    d) all the above   _____

37. What causes poor nail adhesion?
    a) oil and moisture on the nail plate
    b) aggressive filing and improper application techniques
    c) poor-quality products
    d) all the above   _____

38. Identify two types of nail coatings.
    a) polish and acrylic (methacrylate) nail enhancements
    b) resins and nitrocellulose
    c) coatings that cure or polymerize; coatings that evaporate and harden
    d) hard and sticky   _____

39. Nail polishes and top coats undergo a:
    a) chemical reaction by evaporating and hardening
    b) physical reaction by hardening through evaporation
    c) chemical reaction through polymerization
    d) physical reaction by hardening through curing _____

40. By undergoing a chemical process, acrylic (methacrylate) and UV gels:
    a) cure or polymerize
    b) evaporate or harden
    c) polymerize or monomer
    d) polymerize or evaporate _____

41. Keratin is a(n):
    a) monomer
    b) polymer
    c) protein polymer
    d) amino acid _____

42. What is polymerization?
    a) chemical reaction that bonds polymer molecules together to form a much larger molecule or monomer
    b) chemical reaction that bonds monomer molecules together to form a much larger molecule or polymer
    c) physical reaction that bonds polymer molecules together to form a much larger molecule or monomer
    d) physical reaction that bonds monomer molecules together to form a much larger molecule or polymer _____

43. Rapid polymerization causes:
    a) the product to thin
    b) thickening of the product
    c) more room for the product
    d) a shiny surface _____

44. When a polymer chain's growth is halted before it is long enough to become a polymer, it is called a(n):
    a) multimonomer
    b) multimer
    c) minipolymer
    d) oligomer _____

45. Oligomers are used for:
    a) rapid curing of gel nails
    b) speeding up services when you are running behind
    c) all nail enhancement services
    d) all the above _____

46. The sticky surface on UV gels is caused by:
    a) oils
    b) oligomers
    c) UV light
    d) adhesion ingredient _____

47. How do monomers attach to each other?
    a) head of one monomer   b) going tail to tail
       to the tail of another
    c) polymers to each other d) amino acids together _____

48. How are wraps and adhesives formed?
    a) simple monomer   b) simple polymer chains
       chains
    c) helix coils   d) cytokines _____

49. You can unravel simple polymer chains used in wraps and
    adhesives by:
    a) blunt force   b) heavy stress
    c) solvent   d) all the above _____

50. What do cross-linking agents do?
    a) strengthen monolithic b) make wraps more
       structures   brittle
    c) strengthen simple   d) keep adhesion to a
       polymer chains   minimum _____

51. Cross-linking agents are like:
    a) a fishing net   b) rungs of a ladder
    c) wire mesh   d) a knitted fabric _____

52. What do cross-linking agents do for natural and artificial
    nails?
    a) make them more   b) make them more
       durable   resistant to solvents
    c) make them tougher   d) all the above
       and more resilient _____

53. Define volatile solvent.
    a) one that is capable of b) one that evaporates
       pitting the nails   quickly
    c) a solvent that   d) an explosive solvent
       produces no fumes _____

54. When base coats and top coats evaporate, what is left
    behind?
    a) only the color   b) hardened polymer film
    c) durable color   d) smooth surface _____

55. Nail polishes _____ because they do not contain cross-linked polymers.
   a) are best suited for artificial nail enhancement products
   b) lose their luster
   c) smear easily
   d) chip easily   _____

56. A toxic product is only bad or poisonous when:
   a) it is handled improperly
   b) when you inhale the fumes
   c) you touch it
   d) it is consumed   _____

CHAPTER 12: BASICS OF ELECTRICITY

1. Define electricity.
   - a) visible energy
   - b) form of gas
   - c) form of energy
   - d) form of matter _____

2. Sparks and lightning are:
   - a) flow of electrons
   - b) effects of electricity
   - c) negative charged particles
   - d) shocking effects _____

3. Define electric current.
   - a) flow of electricity along a conductor
   - b) voltage
   - c) conduit
   - d) ampere _____

4. Which of the following best describes an insulator?
   - a) complete circuit
   - b) nonconductor
   - c) twisted metal thread
   - d) silk, wood, or glass _____

5. Any substance that _____ is considered to be a conductor.
   - a) produces ions
   - b) separates negatively charged electrons
   - c) conducts ohms
   - d) allows an electrical current to pass through it _____

6. An electric current will not flow through a conductor unless the force (volts) is stronger than the _____ or _____.
   - a) amps, milliamps
   - b) resistance, ohms
   - c) watts, ohms
   - d) current, force _____

7. All substances can be classified as:
   - a) conductors and conduits
   - b) having electrical properties
   - c) conductors or insulators
   - d) cord or cordless _____

8. What are electric wires?
   - a) nonconductors
   - b) generators
   - c) insulators
   - d) conductors _____

9. Why should you never swim in a lake during a lightning storm?
   a) Water contains no ions.
   b) Lake water has a high metallic content.
   c) This is an urban myth.
   d) Ions in water are good conductors of electricity.   _____

10. When a current flows in only one direction, it is called a:
    a) direct current
    b) alternating current
    c) straight current
    d) one-way current   _____

11. Which of the following is (are) true about alternating current?
    a) It flows in one direction and then the other.
    b) It changes direction 60 times a second.
    c) Any appliance that plugs into the wall uses alternating current.
    d) All the above.   _____

12. Water molecules flow through a hose like:
    a) electrons flow through a wire
    b) electrons flow through glass
    c) electricity flows through the atmosphere
    d) all the above   _____

13. What makes electrons flow?
    a) volts
    b) pressure
    c) amperes
    d) watts   _____

14. What kind of electrical current powers flashlights, cellular telephones, and cordless electric files?
    a) alternating current
    b) batteries
    c) direct current
    d) no current of any kind   _____

15. What is a converter?
    a) regulates the amount of electrical output
    b) transforms direct current into alternating current.
    c) does not exist
    d) allows you to control the amount of watts per second   _____

16. How many watts per second will a 40-watt lightbulb use?
    a) 4
    b) 40
    c) 400
    d) 4,000   _____

17. Which of the following reveals the number of watts in a kilowatt?
    a) 100 watts   b) 1,000 watts
    c) 10,000 watts   d) 1,000,000 watts   _____

18. A 1,000-watt (1-kilowatt) hair dryer uses:
    a) 1,000 watts of energy   b) 1,000 watts of energy
       per second   per minute
    c) 10,000 watts of energy   d) 10,000 watts of energy
       per second   per minute   _____

19. What type of substance makes reactions happen quicker?
    a) light   b) catalyst
    c) heat   d) water   _____

20. What is the role of a catalyst?
    a) act like initiators   b) emit ultraviolet rays
    c) absorb energy like a   d) shield the product from
       battery   sunlight   _____

21. UV-light cured enhancements use UV light to produce:
    a) physical effects   b) chemical effects
    c) chemical effects and   d) ultraviolet (UV light)
       kill germs   _____

22. To ensure that your electrical equipment is in good working order, how often should it be inspected?
    a) when you first take it   b) during your annual
       out of the box   inspection
    c) never   d) regularly   _____

23. Careless electrical connections and overloaded circuits can result in a:
    a) burn   b) serious fire
    c) electrical shock   d) all the above   _____

24. A fuse or breaker does what?
    a) prevents excessive   b) prevents excessive
       current from passing   current from passing
       through a circuit   through a wire
    c) maintains a steady   d) minimizes fires
       flow of electricity   _____

25. You cannot overload a circuit by:
    a) using too many appliances at once
    b) using too many appliances at once that are on the same circuit
    c) using electrical appliances on a constant basis
    d) using both plug outlets

    _____

26. What is the difference between a fuse and a circuit breaker?
    a) One is a switch, one blows out or melts.
    b) They both blow out and melt.
    c) There is no difference.
    d) A fuse is a true switch.

    _____

27. What have modern circuit breakers replaced?
    a) silk-wrapped wires
    b) fuses
    c) electrical light switches
    d) outlets

    _____

28. When a circuit breaker pops or turns off, what should you do before resetting?
    a) turn off the appliance
    b) inspect insulation
    c) check all connections
    d) all the above

    _____

29. What is the purpose of the Underwriter's Laboratory (UL) certification?
    a) It rates the number of hours appliances can be safely used before switching off.
    b) It certifies the safety of electrical appliances.
    c) It informs you of the type and number of circuit breakers needed to safely use the appliance.
    d) It is only used when appliances use more than 1,000 watts of power.

    _____

30. What symbol should you look for on appliances before purchasing?
    a) manufacturer's symbol of safety
    b) manufacturer's instruction manual
    c) number of watts
    d) Underwriter's Laboratory (UL) symbol

    _____

31. What is a ground connection?
    a) connection that is buried in the ground
    b) a slightly larger prong
    c) connection that completes the circuit and carries the current safely away to the ground
    d) added protection

    _____

32. Identify the most important advantage of having an extra ground.
    a) It protects you if the first ground fails.
    b) It protects you by splitting the electricity into two paths.
    c) It prevents shocks.
    d) It allows the appliances to work for longer periods of time without overheating.

    _____

33. When you are through using an electrical appliance, you should:
    a) turn it off and unplug it
    b) turn off
    c) make sure it is upright
    d) flip the circuit breaker

    _____

34. How should you disconnect appliances?
    a) pulling on the cord
    b) pulling on the plug
    c) pulling on the appliance
    d) none of the above

    _____

35. When electrical cords become twisted, it could cause:
    a) an inconvenient situation
    b) a short circuit
    c) wires to go haywire.
    d) wires to ground each other

    _____

36. You should avoid contact with water and metal surfaces when using electricity because:
    a) water and metal are conductors
    b) electricity is attracted to water and metal
    c) there is a potential for shock
    d) all the above

    _____

37. You should never place objects on or _____ electric cords.
    a) step over
    b) step on
    c) hide
    d) near

    _____

38. The only time you should attempt to repair an electrical appliance is if:

a) you are qualified and certified

b) it is a simple job

c) you think you know what you are doing

d) there is no one around to help you

_____

CHAPTER 13: MANICURING

1. Which of the following condition(s) would benefit from a conditioning oil manicure?
   - a) brittle nails
   - b) nail ridges
   - c) dry skin around the nail plate
   - d) all the above
   _____

2. Define paraffin.
   - a) a petroleum by-product
   - b) a jellylike substance
   - c) an organic oil
   - d) a non-petroleum form of wax
   _____

3. In men's manicures, what replaces the colored polish step?
   - a) 30-minute massage
   - b) matte top coat or buffing service
   - c) callus removal
   - d) hand softening treatment
   _____

4. What are the contraindications for a paraffin wax treatment?
   - a) sensitivities to heat due to medications or thinning skin
   - b) skin irritations
   - c) impaired circulation
   - d) all the above
   _____

5. Hand-and-arm massage is always done as part of:
   - a) a spa manicure
   - b) a manicure service when clients are stressed
   - c) a slower period of the day
   - d) when the timing seems right
   _____

6. Define effleurage.
   - a) rolling and kneading
   - b) wringing movements
   - c) rapid tapping movements
   - d) long, smooth strokes
   _____

7. When should the massage portion of the manicure be done?
   - a) after the manicure, and before the polish
   - b) at the beginning, and before the client pays
   - c) at the beginning, and after the cuticle remover is applied
   - d) any time
   _____

8. In a regular manicure, what step does a paraffin wax treatment replace?

    a) lotion and massage   b) lotion

    c) nothing   d) polish   _____

9. You can practice sound ergonomics while massaging your clients' hands and feet by:

    a) keeping your legs straight   b) keeping your shoulders level

    c) standing up   d) never leaning toward your client   _____

10. What medical condition(s) are contraindicative of massage?

    a) heart condition   b) high blood pressure

    c) clients who have had, or are at risk for, a stroke   d) all the above   _____

11. Define aromatherapy.

    a) the medical science of well-being   b) botanical essential oils used to promote a sense of well-being

    c) a new-age solution to stress   d) moisturizing oils that deeply penetrate the skin   _____

12. A diamond-cut file has this distinct advantage:

    a) It is superior to ruby files.   b) It does not fill up with debris as quickly.

    c) It holds its value.   d) It can be sanitized.   _____

13. Which of the following describe(s) the function or appearance of a curette?

    a) removes debris under the nail   b) removes cuticle tissue on the surface of the nail

    c) spoon-shaped instrument   d) all the above   _____

14. What is peculiar about a rasp in terms of manual abrasives?

    a) It must be used with warm, soapy water.   b) It can be filed in only one direction.

    c) It is excellent for anyone with sore feet.   d) It removes even the toughest dead skin.   _____

15. Define massage.
    a) kneading and stroking   b) manipulating the body
                                    through a series of
                                    specific movements
    c) percussion   d) tapping and wringing   _____

16. Regular soaps are inferior to antibacterial soaps in terms of
    cleaning and deodorizing the feet.
    a) Yes   b) No
    c) always   d) never   _____

17. Most things that are used once on clients and then discarded
    are called:
    a) equipment   b) implements
    c) materials or supplies   d) cosmetics   _____

18. Identify the implement(s) that are disposable:
    a) acetone   b) nail polish
    c) wooden pusher   d) cotton   _____

19. The recommended wattage for a bulb used in a manicure
    lamp is between _____ watts.
    a) 25 and 30   b) 30 and 35
    c) 40 and 60   d) 60 and 75   _____

20. Nondisposable implements that can be sanitized,
    disinfected, and reused include:
    a) nail clippers   b) tweezers
    c) metal pushers   d) all the above   _____

21. Metal implements must be _____ before being
    disinfected.
    a) cleaned with a towel   b) washed with soap and
                                    water
    c) cleaned in an   d) rinsed in alcohol
       autoclave   _____

22. The implement you use to shape the free edge is called a(n):
    a) wooden pusher   b) abrasive file
    c) metal pusher   d) tweezers   _____

23. What should you do with an implement that is contaminated
    with blood?
    a) rinse with water   b) wipe off with cotton
    c) bag and discard   d) clean and disinfect   _____

24. To remove nail cosmetics from their containers, use a:
     a) wooden pusher   b) metal pusher
     c) plastic or metal spatula d) cotton swab   _____

25. Identify the proper way to immerse implements in a
    disinfectant solution.
     a) wipe thoroughly   b) quickly rinse
     c) fully immerse   d) dip slightly   _____

26. Nail clippers are beneficial when shortening the nail length
    because they:
     a) create a high shine   b) reduce filing time
     c) strengthen weak nails d) reduce splitting   _____

27. The best implement for smoothing out wavy ridges and
    creating a shiny nail plate is a:
     a) nail clipper   b) ridge filler
     c) abrasive file   d) three-way buffer   _____

28. Identify the self-disinfecting product(s):
     a) monomer liquid   b) alcohol
     c) nail polish   d) all the above   _____

29. What is the best way to prevent excessive odors and control
    vapors from nail services in salons?
     a) plastic trash can   b) multiple paper bags
     c) ventilated receptacles d) metal receptacle with
        with lids   self-closing lid   _____

30. Before applying base coat, you must:
     a) apply cuticle remover b) soak the fingers in a
                                  finger bowl
     c) remove all traces of oil d) wash hands
                                  thoroughly   _____

31. A _____ is used to clean fingernails and remove debris.
     a) nail file   b) chamois buffer
     c) wooden pusher   d) nail brush   _____

32. A _____ is used to soften cuticles and increase the
    flexibility of natural nails.
     a) cuticle remover   b) polish remover
     c) penetrating oil   d) nail bleach   _____

33. Key ingredients in nail hardener formulations including nylon, protein, and:
    a) UV gels
    b) formaldehyde
    c) potassium hydroxide
    d) acetone _____

34. Quick-dry nail polish products may be sprayed on or applied with a:
    a) wooden pusher
    b) metal pusher
    c) cotton swab
    d) dropper _____

35. When the free edge has no rounding at the edges and is filed straight across, it is called:
    a) pointed
    b) round
    c) square
    d) squoval _____

36. When the nail extends slightly past the fingertip and is shaped in a gentle c-curve, it is called:
    a) round
    b) pointed
    c) squoval
    d) square _____

37. A top coat or sealer makes nail polish:
    a) dry more quickly
    b) adhere to nail plate
    c) resistant to chipping
    d) bubble free _____

38. Manicures consist of these three parts or segments:
    a) pre-service, service, post-service
    b) actual service, post-service, follow-up
    c) pre-service, post-service, follow-up
    d) pre-service, post-service, product recommendation _____

39. A polish design that has a dramatic _____ on the free edge, is called a French manicure.
    a) peach
    b) pink
    c) white
    d) neutral _____

CHAPTER 14: PEDICURING

1. How often should a client have a pedicure to ensure healthy, happy feet?
   - a) weekly
   - b) daily
   - c) yearly
   - d) monthly

   _____

2. When clients come to their pedicure appointments wearing closed-toed shoes, what should you have them wear afterwards to prevent the polish from being marred or smeared?
   - a) toenail clippers
   - b) pedicure slippers
   - c) toe separators
   - d) pedicure footrest

   _____

3. For your convenience, a pedicure station should be near what?
   - a) sink
   - b) front door
   - c) waiting area
   - d) lounge

   _____

4. What is one of your primary responsibilities toward your clients?
   - a) attitude
   - b) safety
   - c) comfort
   - d) happiness

   _____

5. What is the ideal way to clip the toenails when performing a pedicure?
   - a) extremely short
   - b) long and elegant
   - c) pointed and thinned
   - d) even with end of toe

   _____

6. What is an important part of a pedicure post-service procedure?
   - a) compliment the client
   - b) advise the client
   - c) help the client exit quickly
   - d) soothe the client

   _____

7. What is the name for a fully-plumbed, free-standing pedicure unit?
   - a) pedicure throne
   - b) wet chair
   - c) royal chair
   - d) whirlpool unit

   _____

8. What is a rasp?
   - a) a nail file
   - b) a file used most often used for the sides of the big toe
   - c) a big toe separator
   - d) a multidirectional tool

   _____

9. When massaging the feet and calves, a light or hard stroking movement is called:
   a) effleurage
   b) petrissage
   c) tapotement
   d) percussion _____

10. At a minimum, when should a foot spa be disinfected?
    a) after each use
    b) at the end of each week
    c) at the end of each day
    d) at the end of each month _____

11. In massage, a movement that includes kneading, squeezing, and friction is called:
    a) effleurage
    b) percussion
    c) petrissage
    d) tapotement _____

12. Clients with poor circulation or diabetes must _____ before having a pedicure service.
    a) sign a liability release form
    b) provide a doctor's release
    c) read a pamphlet covering the risks of having a pedicure service
    d) give verbal consent to proceed with service _____

13. The products used in a pedicure bath to soften the skin are called:
    a) foot soaks
    b) foot rubs
    c) foot scrubs
    d) foot masques _____

14. What type of product is used to soften cuticles for removal from the nail plate?
    a) cuticle strengtheners
    b) nail plate dissolvers
    c) cuticle softeners
    d) cuticle removers _____

15. What is the name of the implement with an end that is shaped like an ice cream scooper?
    a) rasp
    b) nail scoop
    c) curette
    d) metal pusher _____

16. How many teaspoons of bleach solution should be used to 5 gallons of water when disinfecting a foot spa?
    a) 1 teaspoon
    b) 4 teaspoons
    c) 2 teaspoons
    d) 1 cup _____

17. What category of products is used to smooth dry, flaky skin and calluses?
    a) massage preparations b) scrubs
    c) sea salts   d) clay masques   _____

18. In foot massage, the metatarsal scissors technique is a _____ movement.
    a) percussion   b) effleurage
    c) petrissage   d) tapotement   _____

19. What percentage of bleach should be used when disinfecting a pedicure bath?
    a) 7%   b) 3%
    c) 5%   d) 2%   _____

20. What does it mean to exfoliate the skin?
    a) remove dead, dry skin b) remove the first layer
                                of skin
    c) remove the stratum   d) rub the skin with a
       corneum   thick oil   _____

21. What is the purpose of a callus softener?
    a) soften and strengthen b) soften and smooth
       calluses, especially   calluses, especially
       on heels and over   on heels and over
       pressure points   pressure points
    c) dissolve skin   d) remove corns and
                                 calluses   _____

22. What is a foot file used for?
    a) to smooth calluses   b) to paddle the soles of
       and remove dry, flaky   the feet as part of a
       skin   percussion massage
    c) to smooth skin on the d) to shape the toenails
       hands and feet   _____

23. Why should a callus never be removed?
    a) A callus is a protective b) It should be removed
       covering.   only by a podiatrist.
    c) It should be dissolved,   d) Callus protects the
       not manually removed.   bones.   _____

24. What are nippers used for?
    a) to remove dead skin   b) to trim the nail
       on the heel
    c) to remove dead tags   d) to remove one layer of
       of skin around the nail   living tissue
       plate   _____

70

25. Which of the following are characteristics of a cuticle remover?

a) highly alkaline, corrosive, and fast acting

b) highly acidic, corrosive, and fast acting

c) highly acidic, noncorrosive, and fast acting

d) highly alkaline, noncorrosive, and fast acting

_____

CHAPTER 15: ELECTRIC FILING

1. Define torque.
   - a) amount of motor resistance
   - b) RPMs
   - c) power of machine's motor
   - d) shank size
   _____

2. Which of these machines is recommended for professional nail technicians?
   - a) micromotor
   - b) belt-driven
   - c) macromotor
   - d) portable drills
   _____

3. Rings of fire are caused by:
   - a) filing too aggressively
   - b) motor running too slowly
   - c) coarse abrasives
   - d) improper angle of bit
   _____

4. What denotes the speed of an electric file?
   - a) miles per hour (MPH)
   - b) revolutions per minute (RPM)
   - c) nanoturns
   - d) high, medium, and low
   _____

5. Concentric bits are important because they:
   - a) do not wobble
   - b) do not heat up as quickly
   - c) are easier to attach
   - d) produce better results
   _____

6. When bits have sharp edges, they should be:
   - a) smoothed with a 240 grit abrasive
   - b) filed while bit is spinning at low speed
   - c) returned to manufacturer
   - d) used until edges become dull
   _____

7. Sander, diamond, _____, and _____, are the four most common types of bits used by salon professionals.
   - a) carbide, Swiss carbide
   - b) tourmaline, ruby
   - c) buffers, filers
   - d) flutes, sleeves
   _____

8. The particles produced by sanders or sleeves (bits):
   - a) require frequent sanitizing of surfaces
   - b) float high and are easily inhaled
   - c) do not pose a health risk
   - d) are healthier to use than metal bits
   _____

9. Carbide bits are unique because they:
    a) have flutes instead of grit
    b) last the longest
    c) are disposable
    d) are the least expensive _____

10. An electric file that has a forward-and-reverse feature is important when:
    a) you are right-handed
    b) you are an expert
    c) you are left-handed
    d) you suffer from wrist fatigue _____

11. The ruby or sapphire particles on pedicure bits are commonly used to:
    a) smooth corns
    b) smooth calluses
    c) remove imbedded dirt
    d) all the above _____

12. It is important to keep the bit _____ when using an electric file.
    a) perpendicular to the table
    b) flat with wrist turned slight downward
    c) flat and parallel with the table
    d) flat and parallel to your shoulders _____

13. Under the free edge, barrel-shaped or tapered Swiss carbide bits are best for:
    a) refining c-curves
    b) making a perfect squoval
    c) squaring nail tips
    d) u-shaped surfaces _____

14. To ensure that an artificial nail enhancement has no visible scratches, you should finish the nail by:
    a) using nail oil
    b) using cream and pumice powder
    c) graduating bits coarse to fine
    d) finishing with a buffer bit _____

15. Which of the following does not cause the bit to grab the nail?
    a) uneven nail surfaces
    b) improper angle of bit
    c) warped bits
    d) coarse grits _____

16. Which of the following describe(s) potential causes of microshattering?
    a) using poor-quality bits
    b) handpiece held at wrong angle
    c) working too aggressively
    d) all the above _____

17. Vibration can cause:
    a) nail tips to crack
    b) damage to fingertips
    c) carpal tunnel syndrome
    d) excessive nervousness

    _____

18. How do you disinfect a metal bit?
    a) You do not; they are disposable.
    b) Disinfect by hand to avoid damage.
    c) Disinfect the same way as any nondisposable implement.
    d) Disinfect while the bit is running.

    _____

19. What does AEFM stand for?
    a) Association of Electric File Manufacturers
    b) Association of Eclectic File Manufacturers
    c) Association of Ergonomic File Manufacturers
    d) Association of Egregious File Manufacturers

    _____

20. Why is the AEFM important to nail technicians?
    a) It is a training organization.
    b) It sets safety standards for the nail industry.
    c) It is product-neutral.
    d) All the above.

    _____

21. An electric file with a closed casing is recommended because:
    a) it is more comfortable to hold
    b) it keeps dust out of the casing and the internal mechanisms
    c) it is a more expensive machine
    d) it prevents air from blowing on your client's hands while working

    _____

22. Why is a keyless feature beneficial to nail technicians?
    a) You can change bits with one hand.
    b) It allows you to use many different kinds of bits.
    c) You do not have to worry about losing your key.
    d) It makes it easier to change bits.

    _____

23. Lighter machines have:
    a) better design
    b) the same amount of power
    c) less power
    d) no power

    _____

74

24. A micromotor machine has a motor that is so small:
    a) it is electric
    b) the motor barely vibrates
    c) it weighs only 5 ounces
    d) it is housed in the handpiece _____

25. The grit of a bit is determined by:
    a) the number of particles that are evenly distributed on the bit
    b) the size and distribution of particles
    c) the type of particles
    d) whether or not it has flutes or particles _____

26. When using sanders or sleeves, the greatest disadvantage is that:
    a) they wear out mid-service
    b) dust particles float in the air and can be inhaled
    c) they tend to grab the nail
    d) they overheat _____

27. Diamond bits that are lower quality:
    a) are less versatile than sanders
    b) may cause scratches on the surface of the nail
    c) tend to skip
    d) are only available in one grit _____

28. Traditional carbide bits:
    a) will skip on the return stroke leaving scratches on the surface of the enhancement
    b) are the same as cross-cut carbide bits
    c) are the same as Swiss carbide bits
    d) are made out of an inferior alloy when compared to Swiss carbide bits _____

29. Some of the characteristics of higher-quality diamond bits are:

a) Construction is more consistent because each particle on every bit is cut the same size and shape and then adhered to a medical stainless steel bit.

b) Seventy percent of the particles are higher-quality diamonds.

c) Each diamond chip is hand assembled on a medical-grade stainless steel metal bit.

d) All diamond chips come from the same stone.

_____

30. When filing the sides of the nail, which bit should you use?
a) cross-cut carbide bit
b) Swiss carbide bit
c) sander or sleeve
d) ruby

_____

31. Describe buffing bits:
a) bits made of soft materials like chamois, leather, or goat's hair
b) bits made of very fine particles
c) disposable cloth bits
d) three-way bits

_____

32. What is the most important benefit of using higher speeds with your electric file?
a) doing a better job
b) working faster
c) applying less pressure
d) working equally well on gels and acrylics (methacrylate)

_____

33. To smooth old product in the regrowth area of the nail, prep this area with a:
a) fine-grit bit
b) medium-grit bit
c) Swiss carbide bit
d) only a diamond bit

_____

34. Why are buffing oils frequently used when using an electric file?

a) They condition the cuticles.

b) They reduce heat and hold dust on the surface of the bit.

c) They create a glossy shine.

d) They enhance smoothness of UV gels if used before applying UV gel sealers.

_____

35. Which bits create the least amount of airborne dust?
    a) sanders and sleeves   b) diamond bits
    c) carbide and Swiss   d) pedicure bits
       carbide bits   _____

36. Any time you find yourself feeling the need to press harder
    on the nail, you should:
    a) press harder   b) reduce speed
    c) be more patient   d) increase speed   _____

CHAPTER 16: NAIL TIPS, WRAPS, AND NO-LIGHT GELS

1. An artificial nail tip is made from what material?
   a) common plastic used   b) tenite acetate polymer
       to make utensils   or ABS
   c) monomer and polymer   d) ceramic   _____

2. An artificial nail product that is used to add length is called
   a(n):
   a) overlay   b) acrylic nail
   c) nail wrap   d) nail tip   _____

3. What is the primary purpose of a nail tip?
   a) repair a damaged nail   b) add length to nail
   c) overlay for gels   d) overlay for acrylic
                                  (methacrylate) nail
                                  enhancements   _____

4. In order for a nail tip to be durable, it must be reinforced
   with a(n):
   a) well   b) resin activator
   c) adhesive   d) overlay   _____

5. When applying a nail tip, an abrasive is used to:
   a) attach the tip   b) attach the wrap
   c) remove the tip   d) remove surface shine   _____

6. The _____ is the point of contact with the nail plate.
   a) nail tip   b) nail well
   c) nail wrap   d) nail resin   _____

7. What should you wear when handling nail adhesive?
   a) face shield   b) gloves
   c) safety eyewear   d) nonabsorbent apron   _____

8. A nail tip should cover no more than _____ of the
   natural nail.
   a) 1/4   b) 1/3
   c) 1/16   d) 1/8   _____

9. Natural oil and shine are removed by using:
   a) antibacterial soap   b) nail wrap material
   c) an abrasive   d) adhesive   _____

10. You attach a nail tip to the nail plate by using:
    a) the stop, rock, and hold procedure
    b) a cotton-tipped wooden pusher
    c) a small nail brush
    d) the stop, rock, and slide procedure _____

11. To create the least amount of damage to the natural nail, you should remove softened nail tips by:
    a) rubbing them off
    b) pulling them off
    c) sliding them off
    d) nipping them off _____

12. A thin, elongated board with a rough surface is called a(n):
    a) abrasive
    b) nipper
    c) buffer
    d) adhesive _____

13. When you bond nail-size pieces of cloth or paper to the top of the nail plate, what service are you performing?
    a) repair patch
    b) UV gel
    c) nail wrap
    d) buffer wrap _____

14. Using a piece of fabric cut to precisely cover a crack in the nail is called a:
    a) nail wrap
    b) repair patch
    c) no-light gel
    d) fiberglass resin _____

15. Which nail wrapping material becomes transparent when adhesive is applied?
    a) silk
    b) linen
    c) satin
    d) cotton _____

16. You can cut nail tips with a special implement called a:
    a) nail clipper
    b) nail cutter
    c) nail nipper
    d) tip cutter _____

17. Acrylic (methacrylate) liquid and powder, wraps, or UV gels are used as _____ on natural nails.
    a) nail tips
    b) overlays
    c) underlays
    d) wraps _____

18. The thickness of adhesive is called:
    a) oil remover
    b) dehydrator
    c) viscosity
    d) polymer _____

19. The product that is designed to remove moisture from the nail plate is called:
    a) a dehydrator
    b) polish thinner
    c) soap and water
    d) cuticle remover _____

20. You can minimize damage to the natural nail when applying nail tips by:
    a) buffing the nail wrap
    b) using a fine abrasive
    c) applying resin activator
    d) preblending the nail tip

    _____

21. The _____ causes UV gel nails to harden.
    a) resin
    b) oil
    c) activator
    d) gel

    _____

22. A perfect nail tip fit:
    a) is the perfect shape
    b) covers the nail plate from sidewall to sidewall
    c) means the tip covers the entire nail perfectly
    d) means the tip is not too long

    _____

23. When you do not have a tip that perfectly fits your client's nail, you should:
    a) glue two tips together
    b) use a larger one and file it down to size
    c) find the closest one that fits
    d) refuse the service

    _____

24. In the stop, rock, and hold method of applying tips, the tip should be held:
    a) with tweezers
    b) at a 45-degree angle
    c) at a 90-degree angle
    d) with your pinkie

    _____

25. The _____ motion is the second step of a nail tip application.
    a) rock
    b) roll
    c) jiggle
    d) freeze

    _____

26. The third step of a nail tip application is to _____ the tip in place.
    a) hold
    b) do not hold
    c) squeeze
    d) press

    _____

27. Identify the safest way(s) to remove a fabric nail wrap.
    a) Soak the nail wrap in an acetone solution until softened.
    b) Slide off the nail wrap using a wooden pusher.
    c) Buff the nail to remove any adhesive residue.
    d) All the above.

    _____

28. What is a nail wrap used for?
    a) to correct spoon-shaped nails
    b) to keep the natural nails in tip-top shape
    c) to lengthen nails
    d) less expensive way to have long beautiful nails _____

29. How should you apply nail adhesive when doing a fabric wrap?
    a) a thin line down the center of the nail
    b) one drop in the center of the nail plate
    c) over the entire nail
    d) only on the nail tip _____

30. A wrap resin should be applied:
    a) down the center of the nail with an extender tip
    b) all over the nail wrap
    c) a drop in the center of the nail
    d) in a crisscross fashion using a nail extender tip _____

31. Between the fabric and the sidewalls, you should leave _____ margin.
    a) a 1/16-inch
    b) a 1/32-inch
    c) a 1/8-inch
    d) no _____

32. Allowing nail adhesive to extend from the nail wrap to the skin can cause:
    a) skin irritation and nail pitting
    b) skin irritation and loose cuticles
    c) skin irritation and lifting
    d) lifting and damaged matrix _____

33. You should maintain fabric wraps every:
    a) 1 week
    b) 2 weeks
    c) month
    d) 6 weeks _____

34. Using an activator with fabric wraps:
    a) makes the wrap stick to the nail plate
    b) makes the fabric more durable
    c) shortens the amount of time it takes to wrap the nails
    d) speeds up the hardening process _____

35. The protocol for a two-week maintenance appointment of fabric wraps involves:

a) applying wrap resin to new nail growth only

b) applying accelerator to the entire nail

c) applying a fresh coat of wrap resin to the entire nail

d) all the above

_____

CHAPTER 17: ACRYLIC (METHACRYLATE) NAIL ENHANCEMENTS

1. Artificial nail enhancements that use a liquid-and-powder system are made of:
   a) acrylic (methacrylate) b) polycrylic
   c) synthetics d) monocrylic _____

2. The technical name for the subcategory of acrylic substances that is used to make nail enhancements is called:
   a) acrylate b) methacrylate
   c) methacrylic d) polyacrylics _____

3. Acrylic nails are a _____-and-powder system.
   a) primer b) liquid
   c) adhesive d) powder _____

4. The polymer in acrylic nail enhancements is in the:
   a) powder b) dehydrator
   c) liquid d) adhesive _____

5. A monomer unit is made up of one:
   a) primer b) initiator
   c) catalyst d) molecule _____

6. The monomer liquid portion of acrylic nails consists of which substance?
   a) isopropyl methacrylate b) benzoyl peroxide
   c) methacrylate d) ethyl alcohol _____

7. Acrylic (methacrylate) nail enhancements are hardened by a chemical process called:
   a) rebalancing b) polymerization
   c) molecular hardening d) initiation _____

8. Surface moisture is removed from the nails prior to an acrylic (methacrylate) service by using a:
   a) dehydrator b) initiator
   c) primer d) catalyst _____

9. The chemical reaction is accelerated by using a(n):
   a) dehydrator b) catalyst
   c) primer d) initiator _____

10. The product used to remove surface moisture from the nails prior to an acrylic nail application is called a(n):
    a) dehydrator　　　　　　b) initiator
    c) primer　　　　　　　　d) catalyst　　　　＿＿＿＿

11. Which product is used to ensure strong adhesion and prevent lifting problems with acrylic (methacrylate) nails?
    a) dehydrator　　　　　　b) initiator
    c) primer　　　　　　　　d) catalyst　　　　＿＿＿＿

12. A polymer chain is created by a ＿＿＿＿＿＿ that causes monomers to chemically link together.
    a) rebalancing　　　　　　b) molecular reaction
    c) chain reaction　　　　　d) chemical reaction　＿＿＿＿

13. The set or cure time is controlled by catalysts that are added to the:
    a) adhesive　　　　　　　b) catalyst
    c) powder　　　　　　　　d) liquid　　　　　＿＿＿＿

14. Benzoyl peroxide is a(n) ＿＿＿＿＿＿ that is added to the powder to start a chain reaction that leads to long polymer chains.
    a) initiator　　　　　　　b) catalyst
    c) dehydrator　　　　　　d) primer　　　　　＿＿＿＿

15. When you use the wrong powder with your chosen liquid, your artificial nail enhancements could be:
    a) too brittle　　　　　　b) too flimsy
    c) improperly cured　　　d) all the above　　＿＿＿＿

16. The amount of liquid and powder used to create an acrylic bead is called the:
    a) wet bead　　　　　　　b) dry bead
    c) medium bead　　　　　d) mix ratio　　　　＿＿＿＿

17. Which mix ratio is needed to create a medium bead?
    a) twice as much liquid　b) equal parts
    　　as powder
    c) 1/2 more powder than　d) 3/4 liquid to 1/4 powder
    　　liquid　　　　　　　　　　　　　　　　　＿＿＿＿

18. An acrylic bead is created by doing what?
    a) mixing powder and　　b) dipping brush in liquid,
    　　liquid　　　　　　　　　then in powder
    c) dipping brush in　　　d) combining liquid and
    　　powder and then　　　　powder in a dappen
    　　liquid　　　　　　　　　dish　　　　　　　＿＿＿＿

19. The three types of bead mix ratios are:
    a) wet, medium, dry   b) thin, medium, thick
    c) loose, medium, set   d) runny, medium, hard   _____

20. The ideal mix ratio for working with monomer liquids and
polymer powders:
    a) is generally dry   b) is generally medium
    c) is generally wet   d) depends on the type
                              of enhancement you
                              are forming   _____

21. You must use the correct mixture of powder and liquid in
order to ensure the proper set and maximum _____ of
the nail enhancement.
    a) resiliency   b) durability
    c) adaptability   d) beauty   _____

22. If too little powder is used, a nail enhancement can be:
    a) discolored   b) too strong
    c) rubbery   d) weak   _____

23. A(n) _____ primer is corrosive to the skin and
potentially dangerous to the eyes.
    a) alkaline-based   b) acid-based
    c) monomer-based   d) alcohol-based   _____

24. The most important benefit of using a dappen dish is that it:
    a) minimizes fumes   b) maximizes
                              evaporation
    c) minimizes   d) maximizes
       condensation   condensation   _____

25. When applying acrylic nail enhancements, the best brush
bristle is made of:
    a) sable hair   b) synthetic fiber
    c) mink hair   d) bristle fiber   _____

26. _____ gloves work best for nail-related applications.
    a) Nitrile polyester   b) Nitrile polymer
    c) Benzoyl polymer   d) Benzoyl polyester   _____

27. When tapped with the end of your brush, acrylic nail
enhancements will make a clicking sound when they are
hard enough to:
    a) nip and trim   b) polish and finish
    c) clip and trim   d) file and shape   _____

28. Nail enhancements that are not properly maintained have a greater tendency to:
    a) grow and strengthen
    b) lift and break
    c) grow slower
    d) split and chip
    _____

29. The beauty, durability, and longevity of an artificial nail enhancement are achieved through this maintenance service:
    a) refreshing
    b) servicing
    c) rebalancing
    d) restructuring
    _____

30. You can cause lifting problems and possible damage to the _____ by nipping off acrylic material, whether it is loose or attached to the nail.
    a) nail bed
    b) hyponychium
    c) eponychium
    d) matrix
    _____

31. Odorless acrylic (methacrylate) nail enhancement products harden more slowly and form a(n) _____ layer on top of the nail.
    a) exhibition
    b) sticky
    c) inhibition
    d) assertion
    _____

32. Which motion is required to create the proper mix of powder and liquid with low-odor acrylic (methacrylate) products?
    a) multiple circular motions
    b) single dip
    c) multiple vertical dipping motions
    d) minimal circular motions
    _____

33. Low-odor products generally require which type of bead mix ratio?
    a) dry
    b) wet
    c) medium
    d) hard
    _____

34. Odorless acrylic products have the same chemical composition as regular acrylic products except they rely on _____ that have little odor.
    a) monomers
    b) polymers
    c) acid primers
    d) catalysts
    _____

35. Odorless products _____ more slowly, and form a(n) _____ layer.
    a) harden, exhibition
    b) cure, sticky
    c) cure, tacky
    d) harden, inhibition
    _____

36. You should always _____ when filing away the inhibition
    layer of a low-odor acrylic product.
    a) wear a mask   b) avoid contact with the
                                   freshly filed particles
    c) use a disposable file   d) Never file away these
                                   particles.   _____

37. When you rewet your brush with monomer after applying the
    acrylic bead to the nail, you risk:
    a) cross-contamination   b) diluting the product
    c) using this method as a   d) always producing an
       crutch   inferior result   _____

CHAPTER 18: UV GELS

1. UV gel enhancements rely on what family of ingredients?
   - a) wrap resin
   - b) adhesives
   - c) fiberglass
   - d) acrylic
   _____

2. Which ingredients in UV gels cut the curing time from 3 hours to 3 minutes?
   - a) monomers
   - b) oligomers
   - c) polymers
   - d) primers
   _____

3. What sets UV gel nail enhancements apart from all other nail enhancements?
   - a) soaking
   - b) clipping
   - c) filing
   - d) curing
   _____

4. Urethane acrylate and urethane methacrylate are responsible for making what?
   - a) fiberglass wraps
   - b) UV gels
   - c) sculptured nails
   - d) nail tips
   _____

5. How do you measure the amount of electricity that UV bulbs consume?
   - a) voltages
   - b) amperes
   - c) ohms
   - d) wattage
   _____

6. What applicator is used to spread UV gel product onto the nail?
   - a) synthetic brushes
   - b) natural brushes
   - c) wooden pushers
   - d) metal pushers
   _____

7. Adhesion of UV gels to the natural nail plate is enhanced by using this product:
   - a) UV gel glue
   - b) UV gel primer
   - c) UV gel paste
   - d) UV gel buffer
   _____

8. What is the proper term for dipping the tip of the applicator brush into nail primer to ensure that the nail plate is covered?
   - a) priming the tip
   - b) dehydrating the eponychium
   - c) natural nail preparation
   - d) conditioning the nail
   _____

9. UV gel #1 is referred to as the:
   - a) base coat gel
   - b) primer coat gel
   - c) builder gel
   - d) sealer gel
   _____

10. The tacky surface layer of a UV gel nail enhancement is called the _____ layer.
    a) contour
    b) integumentary
    c) aggressive
    d) inhibition
    _____

11. When contouring a UV gel nail, what grit should you be using?
    a) coarse
    b) medium
    c) very fine
    d) metal
    _____

12. What happens when you expose your UV gel product to sunlight, full-spectrum manicure light, or UV gel lamp before you are ready to cure the gel nail?
    a) Product will soften.
    b) Product will thicken.
    c) Product will harden.
    d) Product will liquefy.
    _____

13. UV gel #3 is referred to as:
    a) base coat gel
    b) primer coat gel
    c) builder gel
    d) sealer gel
    _____

14. UV gels should be rebalanced:
    a) every month
    b) every week
    c) when they need it
    d) every 2 to 3 weeks
    _____

15. What is the best way to remove UV gels?
    a) reducing thickness with medium grit abrasive
    b) soaking in acetone to soften product
    c) gently scraping them off using a wooden pusher
    d) all the above
    _____

16. Every layer of a UV gel nail enhancement must:
    a) have sealer applied
    b) nothing
    c) be exposed to UV light
    d) be allowed to air dry
    _____

17. Oligomers are in between _____ and _____.
    a) a medium, strong hold product
    b) a liquid, a gel
    c) monomers, polymers
    d) a liquid, a solid
    _____

18. UV gel #2 is referred to as:
    a) builder UV gel
    b) base coat UV gel
    c) inhibition layer
    d) finisher UV gel
    _____

19. When handling the tacky layer of the UV gel, what precaution(s) apply?
    a) Avoid skin contact.
    b) Nail should be scrubbed.
    c) No precautions are needed.
    d) All tacky material must be removed.   _____

20. _____ are made from either urethane acrylate or urethane methacrylate.
    a) Oligomers
    b) Monomers
    c) Polymers
    d) Primer   _____

21. Which answer most accurately describes UV gel odor?
    a) very little odor
    b) strong odor
    c) no odor
    d) depends on the brand   _____

22. For best results, it is important to:
    a) use the strongest bulb you can find
    b) cure the nails for additional time
    c) change your bulbs every other week
    d) use the lamp designed for your UV gel nail system   _____

23. UV bulbs need to be changed when:
    a) they are no longer blue
    b) they flicker
    c) your clients' nails are not curing properly
    d) you follow a regular replacement schedule   _____

24. What are you risking when you undercure UV gel nails?
    a) service breakdown
    b) skin irritation
    c) client defection
    d) all the above   _____

25. UV gels are _____ acrylics.
    a) harder than
    b) softer than
    c) the same as
    d) cannot compare the two   _____

CHAPTER 19: THE CREATIVE TOUCH

1. Why should you get involved in nail art?
   - a) It is creative.
   - b) It sets your work apart.
   - c) It is an effective marketing tool.
   - d) All the above.

   _____

2. Being open-minded, exposing yourself to all avenues of art services, always listening to your clients, and _____ are the guiding rules of nail art.
   - a) there are no such things as mistakes
   - b) find a design you like and stick to it
   - c) play it safe with your designs
   - d) always push the envelope

   _____

3. Competitively pricing your nail art begins with:
   - a) doing additional art steps at no charge
   - b) learning what other technicians are charging
   - c) using more than one color
   - d) charging $5 less

   _____

4. Polished nails should always be _____ before applying artwork.
   - a) slightly wet
   - b) recleaned
   - c) completely dry
   - d) opaque

   _____

5. The circular color guides that show primary, secondary, tertiary, and complementary colors are called:
   - a) color combinations
   - b) color gradations
   - c) color wheels
   - d) color palettes

   _____

6. The four color classifications of the color wheel are: primary, secondary, tertiary, and:
   - a) analogous
   - b) complementary
   - c) complimentary
   - d) pastel combinations

   _____

7. Define complementary colors.
   - a) a color scheme incorporating opposite hues on the color wheel
   - b) a color scheme incorporating similar hues on the color wheel
   - c) a color palette involving colors that make each other look great
   - d) a color palette of clashing colors

   _____

8. The midsection of the bristles is called the:
   a) thorax
   b) sternum
   c) abdomen
   d) belly
   _____

9. The metal band surrounding the brush is called a:
   a) bracelet
   b) ferrule
   c) brace
   d) brush belly
   _____

10. To apply small gemstones to the nail, use a wooden or metal pusher wrapped in cotton and dipped in:
    a) nail art glue
    b) base coat
    c) nail art polish
    d) nail art sealer
    _____

11. When doing a foiling technique, you begin by applying:
    a) ordinary household glue
    b) base coat
    c) a thin coat of foil adhesive
    d) nail wrap adhesive
    _____

12. Another name for a gold leafing sheet is a:
    a) nugget sheet
    b) leaf
    c) nugget foil
    d) tissue foil
    _____

13. A basic set of brushes is made up of liner, striper, round, fan, and _____ brushes.
    a) detailer and pointer
    b) flat and detailer
    c) square and flat
    d) detailer and nondetailer
    _____

14. When you pull the brush across the paint surface, what do you create?
    a) fluid strokes
    b) wider stripe
    c) crisp line
    d) uneven results
    _____

15. When using an airbrush device, compressed air is drawn from:
    a) an oxygen container
    b) the room
    c) carbon dioxide
    d) outside the salon
    _____

16. The best airbrush system for doing nail art is a _____ system.
    a) bottom feed
    b) dual turbo
    c) gravity fed
    d) battery operated
    _____

17. When you are airbrushing properly, the stream of paint is:
    a) highly visible
    b) rich in color
    c) invisible
    d) noticeably thick
    _____

18. Once you are able to _____, you are ready to practice airbrushing on plastic nails.
    - a) paint with no overspray
    - b) place a dot in the center of a square
    - c) draw a straight grid
    - d) create thick and thin lines   _____

19. When airbrushing, you should:
    - a) brace the gun with your wrist and forearm
    - b) move your arm, but keep your wrist straight
    - c) bend your wrist, keep your arm straight
    - d) move only your wrist   _____

20. When applying paint on the nails correctly, the paint should appear:
    - a) dull and powdery
    - b) slightly iridescent
    - c) shiny and lustrous
    - d) wet looking   _____

21. What is double loading?
    - a) placing two colors in a reservoir
    - b) two colors, one on either side of the brush
    - c) marbleizing
    - d) double dipping   _____

22. The top secret for selling nail art is:
    - a) encouraging clients to be more creative
    - b) giving away nail art for the first three months
    - c) never practicing on clients
    - d) introducing the right design to the right client   _____

23. The end of the brush bristle is called the:
    - a) point
    - b) tip
    - c) ferrule
    - d) belly   _____

24. How do you create a tertiary color?
    - a) Mix equal parts of two primary colors and its nearest secondary color.
    - b) Mix equal parts of one primary color and one of its nearest secondary colors.
    - c) Mix equal parts of two primary colors and the farthest secondary color.
    - d) Mix any three colors.   _____

25. You can create a secondary color by:
    a) mixing equal parts of two tertiary colors
    b) mixing pure pigments together
    c) mixing equal parts of two primary colors together
    d) mixing colors next to each other on the color wheel _____

26. What are primary colors?
    a) Red, blue, and yellow.
    b) Primary colors are pure pigments that are the basis of all other colors.
    c) Primary colors result from mixing equal parts of secondary colors.
    d) Primary colors are pure pigments that are obtained only by mixing other colors together. _____

27. Define color theory.
    a) a science that categorizes colors
    b) system that categorizes colors, and how they relate, blend, and complement each other
    c) describes the effects of light and dark and all colors in the universe
    d) artistic interpretation of colors and how they relate to each other _____

28. An air compressor does not contain a:
    a) compressor
    b) gun
    c) reservoir
    d) brush _____

29. The most common air pressure used to create nail art is:
    a) 25 to 35 pounds psi (per square inch)
    b) 25 to 35 mph (miles per hour)
    c) 25 to 35 RPMs (revolutions per minute)
    d) 100 cubic feet _____

30. You should hold the nozzle _____ from the nail.
    a) 3 to 4 inches
    b) 6 inches
    c) 1 inch
    d) 2 to 3 inches _____

31. An airbrush system works by:
    a) combining air and paint to form an atomized spray
    b) using straight air that has been compressed very tightly
    c) combining oxygen and water to form an atomized spray
    d) combining air from the room and carbon dioxide that we exhale _____

32. Before applying _____, allow the artwork to dry completely.
    a) top coat
    b) nail art sealer
    c) ridge filler
    d) primer _____

33. Floating the bead means:
    a) dropping a generous bead of sealer on the nail plate and floating it across the nail with a brush
    b) forming a very lightweight bead
    c) making the bead perfectly round
    d) using a beaded brush to apply top coat _____

34. No matter how outstanding your work may be, it must fit your clients' _____ and _____.
    a) lifestyle, please their significant other
    b) lifestyle, sense of fashion
    c) lifestyle, comfort zone
    d) mind-set, mood _____

35. Besides _____, doing nail art can be fun and exciting.
    a) preventing your income from declining
    b) dramatically improving your income
    c) maintaining a steady income
    d) enhancing your income _____

CHAPTER 20: SEEKING EMPLOYMENT

1. One of the most important parts of your portfolio is your:
    a) introduction
    b) credit history
    c) employment history
    d) skills inventory
    _____

2. When securing employment, one of your most vital tools is your:
    a) personal background
    b) business portfolio
    c) employment history
    d) personal history
    _____

3. Before you can determine where you want to work in the beauty industry, what should you do?
    a) Send out résumés.
    b) Get a manicure at all targeted salons.
    c) Define career goals.
    d) Attend classes.
    _____

4. When looking for the right salon, what type of clientele should you be seeking?
    a) those with lots of money
    b) one you are comfortable with
    c) conservative and rigid
    d) trendy and avant-garde
    _____

5. What is one of the first things you should do when beginning your job search?
    a) Call a few salons.
    b) Obtain a list of area salons.
    c) Talk to fellow students.
    d) Call for a nail appointment.
    _____

6. When observing the salon, you should notice whether nail technicians are:
    a) professional and well groomed
    b) color-coordinated
    c) maintaining their nail stations
    d) wearing uniforms
    _____

7. If you are seeking immediate employment, when should you start your job search?
    a) When a salon has an ad in the paper.
    b) When you are licensed.
    c) While you are still a student.
    d) When it is the busy season.
    _____

8. One way to determine the type of market a salon is servicing is to:

    a) watch local television   b) drive by the salon regularly

    c) study trade journals   d) watch the salon's advertising   _____

9. What are potential employers most concerned with?

    a) your life insurance policy   b) getting his/her nails done

    c) building a clientele and selling retail   d) keeping records and doing your family's nails   _____

10. When you wait until the last minute to look for your first job, what are you most likely to do?

    a) take the first offer   b) never go to state board

    c) change careers   d) get the best position available   _____

11. Your résumé should be how long?

    a) one-half page   b) one to two pages

    c) no less than three pages   d) as long as necessary   _____

12. What should be the primary focus of your résumé?

    a) secondary education   b) work-related experience

    c) employment record   d) achievements and accomplishments   _____

13. When you are preparing for a job interview, what should you be concerned with?

    a) your wardrobe and overall appearance   b) what the interviewer is wearing

    c) best time of day   d) whether or not to smoke   _____

14. Which of the following questions are illegal to ask during an interview?

    a) religion   b) race

    c) national origin   d) all the above   _____

15. What is the maximum length of time you should take to answer an interviewer's question?

    a) 1 minute   b) all the time you need to explain yourself fully

    c) 3 minutes   d) 2 minutes   _____

16. In a multiple-choice test, when two choices are worded differently but say the same thing, they both must be:
    a) correct   b) incorrect
    c) acceptable   d) logical   _____

17. What is the stem of a question?
    a) basic question   b) challenge
    c) answer   d) nothing important   _____

18. What is the best way to prepare for an exam?
    a) cramming the morning b) avoiding studying two
       of the test   days before
    c) playing mood music   d) avoiding cramming the
       while studying   night before   _____

19. Preparing for a test by practicing good time management skills and having good study habits is called:
    a) being organized   b) being test-wise
    c) being obsessive   d) being test-anxious   _____

20. After interviewing, how should you contact the interviewer and/or owner?
    a) Write a thank-you   b) Drop him/her an email
       note.   to say "Hi."
    c) Send him/her your   d) Talk to the receptionist
       picture.   to find out how you
                         did.   _____

1. It is important to find a salon that:
   a) pays the highest wage b) expects minimum-quality work for new hires
   c) supports your business growth d) stresses advanced education _____

2. Which entry-level job is appropriate for a newly licensed employee?
   a) manager b) employee trainer
   c) entry-level nail technician d) nail director _____

3. You should always put your clients:
   a) last b) on your list of important things
   c) near the top of your priorities d) first _____

4. You are acting respectfully toward your clients and _____ by being punctual and arriving ready to begin work.
   a) neighbors b) husband
   c) coworkers d) children _____

5. Which of the following pertains to your job description?
   a) duties and responsibilities b) calendar of activities
   c) schedule of time off d) personal budget _____

6. When taking your first job, the best type of compensation is:
   a) tips plus salary b) salary plus commission
   c) cash d) straight commission _____

7. Tips are:
   a) taxable up to $400 b) declared but not taxed
   c) reported as income d) not declared or taxed _____

8. A _____ is a formal job review.
   a) job referral b) client feedback form
   c) performance evaluation d) coworker comment sheet _____

9. Developing excellent work habits and skills by choosing a role model:
   a) may be limiting
   b) may be competitive
   c) diminishes who are you
   d) is helpful to becoming excellent in your own right

   _____

10. Striving to help, pitch in, share knowledge, and remain positive are all signs of a:
    a) team player
    b) complainer
    c) problem solver
    d) good client

    _____

11. The best way to estimate income and keep track of expenses is by having:
    a) a mortgage
    b) a tax return
    c) a budget
    d) a retirement plan

    _____

12. Raising your prices on an annual basis does what?
    a) loses clients
    b) helps to keep pace with inflation
    c) loses money
    d) lets you know you have arrived

    _____

13. You are _____ when you do not pay back a loan as promised.
    a) in default
    b) in good standing
    c) depressed
    d) efficient

    _____

14. Once a client has decided to purchase a product, stop:
    a) mentioning benefits
    b) talking
    c) smiling
    d) pointing

    _____

15. When you have your client book his or her next appointment before leaving the salon, you are:
    a) prebooking
    b) rebooking
    c) marketing
    d) referring

    _____

16. You are _____ when you recommend the right retail products.
    a) hard selling
    b) soft selling
    c) thinking about your retail commission
    d) practicing good client care

    _____

17. Your _____ consists of clients that see you on a regular basis.
    a) core clients
    b) clientele
    c) fundamental clients
    d) followers

    _____

18. You can only become a proficient salesperson when you act:
    a) eager
    b) confidently
    c) aggressively
    d) assertively
    _____

19. Define upselling.
    a) ticket upgrading
    b) increasing the number of services
    c) selling for the future
    d) not letting a client leave without buying a product
    _____

20. In a salon situation, you must put the needs of the _____ and _____ first.
    a) salon, clients
    b) salon, coworkers
    c) salon, receptionist
    d) manager, salon
    _____

21. In the salon, scheduling is _____ to the day-to-day operations of the business.
    a) central
    b) everything
    c) peripheral
    d) not so important
    _____

22. Even the most ideal job will have its:
    a) heartbreak
    b) pain
    c) benefits
    d) challenges
    _____

23. You can perfect your _____ while working in a salon.
    a) life skills
    b) customer care skills
    c) salon skills
    d) self skills
    _____

24. Team members realize that you cannot fulfill your work potential:
    a) with a group
    b) alone
    c) without a manager
    d) without walk-ins
    _____

25. You must have _____ in order to perform your duties and do what is expected of you.
    a) a list of recommended classes
    b) a copy of your appointments
    c) good communication
    d) a written job description
    _____

CHAPTER 22: THE SALON BUSINESS

1. The best form of advertising is:
   - a) Yellow Pages
   - b) Internet
   - c) word of mouth
   - d) television
   _____

2. The receptionist is called the quarterback of the salon because:
   - a) a receptionist physically directs the flow of the salon
   - b) a receptionist intercepts problems
   - c) a receptionist makes a game plan for the day
   - d) all the above
   _____

3. What is word-of-mouth advertising?
   - a) free advertisement
   - b) personal recommendation
   - c) a way to build a clientele by pleasing one client after another
   - d) all the above
   _____

4. Each of the following describes entrepreneurial situations except:
   - a) booth rental
   - b) partnership
   - c) sole proprietor
   - d) head nail technician
   _____

5. As a booth renter, you are responsible for all of the following except:
   - a) paying for all education
   - b) managing and paying for inventory
   - c) paying all taxes, including higher Social Security
   - d) maintaining the salon
   _____

6. Two important elements that create a successful salon are:
   - a) having good visibility and accessibility
   - b) having all your supplies paid for and your first month's rent covered
   - c) having cheap rent and no set store hours
   - d) offering quick turnaround on services and promising to do a great job
   _____

7. What is a business plan?
   a) written description of your business as you see it today and as you foresee it in the next 5 years (detailed by year)
   b) written description of your hopes and dreams for your business and where you want to be in 5 years
   c) written description of your business as you see it today and as you believe it will be in the next 5 years
   d) a plan of success that begins with writing down short-term and long-term goals, followed by a goal-setting exercise and a time management program to make them come true _____

8. Identify which of the following is not a business model:
   a) corporation
   b) partnership
   c) sole proprietorship
   d) mayoral department _____

9. A corporation helps protect:
   a) a person's reputation
   b) personal assets
   c) a person's future career
   d) all business assets _____

10. In the event you incur unmanageable debts, a corporation will:
    a) limit monthly payments
    b) limit personal financial liability
    c) protect you from your creditors
    d) prevent you from running into financial trouble _____

11. When purchasing an existing salon, you must have a written agreement that includes:
    a) complete and signed statement of inventory, including the value of each article
    b) written purchase and sale agreement
    c) written agreement of responsibility of existing debt
    d) all the above _____

12. Most salon owners do not own:
    a) the building
    b) their business name
    c) their inventory
    d) their fixtures _____

13. In your lease, you must specify:
    a) who owns the property b) whether or not
       (stations, etc.) that is   you are able to
       physically attached to   sublease your space
       your space.   to an independent
                             contractor or new
                             owner
    c) who is responsible   d) all the above
       for necessary
       renovations and
       regular maintenance
       of the building and
       grounds   _____

14. When purchasing a salon, what information should be
    included about the existing clientele?
    a) client contact list   b) service and visitation
                             records
    c) chemical formulas   d) all the above   _____

15. When you first become a salon owner, it is wise to have a
    _____ who can give you advice along the way.
    a) circle of mentors   b) circle of friends
    c) group of paid   d) circle of salon owners
       consultants   _____

16. A smooth business operation has:
    a) excellent customer   b) sufficient investment
       service delivery and   capital and efficiency
       proper pricing of   of management
       services
    c) trained salon   d) all the above
       personnel and good
       business procedures   _____

17. Your bookkeeping system must keep track of:
    a) service sales   b) retail sales
    c) income and expenses d) employee attendance _____

18. Client service records should include:

a) dates of visits, services received, formulas, retail purchases, client feedback, and any special products used for the services

b) dates of visits and services received

c) dates of visits, services, retail purchases, and whether or not they were prebooked

d) formulas

_____

19. To own a successful salon, your business must:

a) be sparkling clean, be physically attractive, and run smoothly

b) be the most popular in the area

c) be the most progressive

d) have the best receptionist

_____

20. Layout is crucial to having:

a) a profitable salon

b) a physically smooth running operation

c) a happy clientele

d) an injury-free situation

_____

Part II: Answers to Chapter Review Tests

CHAPTER 1: HISTORY AND OPPORTUNITIES

1. a	5. c	9. d	13. a	17. d
2. b	6. d	10. a	14. a	
3. d	7. d	11. a	15. b	
4. c	8. a	12. b	16. d	

CHAPTER 2: LIFE SKILLS

1. d	7. a	13. c	19. b	25. b
2. a	8. b	14. d	20. b	26. b
3. a	9. d	15. a	21. d	27. b
4. d	10. d	16. a	22. c	28. d
5. b	11. d	17. b	23. a	29. b
6. d	12. d	18. a	24. c	30. c

CHAPTER 3: YOUR PROFESSIONAL IMAGE

1. c	7. a	13. b	19. a	25. d
2. a	8. b	14. c	20. b	26. c
3. d	9. d	15. d	21. a	27. b
4. c	10. a	16. d	22. d	
5. d	11. c	17. b	23. c	
6. d	12. a	18. c	24. c	

CHAPTER 4: COMMUNICATING FOR SUCCESS

1. b	6. a	11. c	16. a	21. b
2. b	7. c	12. a	17. c	22. b
3. d	8. b	13. d	18. b	23. b
4. d	9. d	14. b	19. d	24. a
5. b	10. a	15. c	20. c	25. d

CHAPTER 5: INFECTION CONTROL: PRINCIPLES AND PRACTICE

1. a	8. d	15. a	22. a	29. a
2. b	9. b	16. a	23. a	30. d
3. c	10. d	17. c	24. b	31. a
4. a	11. c	18. a	25. b	32. d
5. b	12. c	19. b	26. a	33. a
6. c	13. b	20. d	27. d	34. d
7. a	14. b	21. c	28. b	35. c

CHAPTER 6: GENERAL ANATOMY AND PHYSIOLOGY

1. c	13. a	25. d	37. c	49. a
2. d	14. a	26. c	38. d	50. a
3. b	15. c	27. b	39. c	51. c
4. c	16. a	28. b	40. a	52. a
5. b	17. a	29. d	41. b	53. c
6. a	18. c	30. b	42. d	54. d
7. a	19. b	31. a	43. b	55. b
8. a	20. a	32. d	44. d	56. a
9. c	21. b	33. d	45. b	57. b
10. d	22. c	34. b	46. c	58. b
11. b	23. a	35. d	47. c	59. b
12. b	24. a	36. b	48. b	60. b

CHAPTER 7: SKIN STRUCTURE AND GROWTH

1. d	10. b	19. c	28. d	37. d
2. a	11. b	20. a	29. b	38. d
3. a	12. d	21. c	30. d	39. a
4. a	13. a	22. b	31. a	40. b
5. d	14. b	23. b	32. c	41. c
6. c	15. c	24. c	33. d	42. d
7. d	16. a	25. d	34. c	43. d
8. a	17. d	26. c	35. b	44. c
9. b	18. d	27. b	36. b	

CHAPTER 8: NAIL STRUCTURE AND GROWTH

1. b	7. c	13. c	19. c
2. b	8. d	14. a	20. d
3. d	9. d	15. a	21. a
4. b	10. b	16. a	22. d
5. d	11. b	17. d	23. b
6. b	12. d	18. a	24. a

CHAPTER 9: NAIL DISEASES AND DISORDERS

1. b	9. a	17. d	25. d	33. b
2. d	10. d	18. d	26. b	34. a
3. a	11. b	19. c	27. c	35. d
4. c	12. d	20. d	28. d	36. d
5. b	13. c	21. c	29. c	37. c
6. a	14. a	22. b	30. b	
7. d	15. b	23. a	31. b	
8. c	16. c	24. b	32. d	

CHAPTER 10: BASICS OF CHEMISTRY

1. b	8. d	15. a	22. d	29. c
2. b	9. a	16. b	23. b	30. d
3. a	10. b	17. a	24. c	31. c
4. b	11. a	18. d	25. a	32. b
5. d	12. d	19. b	26. d	33. d
6. b	13. d	20. c	27. b	34. a
7. b	14. b	21. a	28. b	35. b

CHAPTER 11: NAIL PRODUCT CHEMISTRY SIMPLIFIED

1. b	13. a	25. a	37. d	49. d
2. a	14. d	26. a	38. c	50. c
3. d	15. d	27. d	39. b	51. b
4. b	16. b	28. b	40. a	52. d
5. a	17. d	29. a	41. c	53. b
6. c	18. c	30. a	42. b	54. b
7. a	19. a	31. b	43. b	55. d
8. a	20. c	32. b	44. d	56. a
9. d	21. c	33. b	45. a	
10. a	22. d	34. c	46. b	
11. b	23. a	35. a	47. a	
12. b	24. b	36. d	48. b	

CHAPTER 12: BASICS OF ELECTRICITY

1. c	9. d	17. b	25. c	33. a
2. b	10. a	18. a	26. a	34. b
3. a	11. d	19. b	27. b	35. b
4. b	12. a	20. c	28. d	36. d
5. d	13. b	21. c	29. b	37. b
6. b	14. c	22. d	30. d	38. a
7. c	15. b	23. d	31. c	
8. d	16. b	24. a	32. a	

CHAPTER 13: MANICURING

1. d	9. d	17. c	25. c	33. b
2. a	10. d	18. c	26. b	34. d
3. b	11. b	19. c	27. d	35. c
4. d	12. b	20. d	28. d	36. a
5. a	13. d	21. b	29. d	37. c
6. d	14. b	22. b	30. c	38. a
7. a	15. b	23. d	31. d	39. c
8. a	16. b	24. c	32. c	

CHAPTER 14: PEDICURING

1. d	6. b	11. c	16. b	21. b
2. b	7. a	12. b	17. b	22. a
3. a	8. b	13. a	18. c	23. a
4. b	9. a	14. d	19. c	24. c
5. d	10. a	15. c	20. a	25. a

CHAPTER 15: ELECTRIC FILING

1. c	9. a	17. c	25. a	33. b
2. a	10. c	18. c	26. b	34. b
3. d	11. b	19. a	27. b	35. c
4. b	12. c	20. d	28. a	36. d
5. a	13. a	21. b	29. a	
6. b	14. c	22. d	30. b	
7. a	15. d	23. c	31. a	
8. b	16. d	24. d	32. c	

CHAPTER 16: NAIL TIPS, WRAPS, AND NO-LIGHT GELS

1. b	8. b	15. a	22. b	29. b
2. d	9. c	16. d	23. b	30. a
3. b	10. a	17. b	24. b	31. a
4. d	11. c	18. c	25. a	32. c
5. d	12. a	19. a	26. a	33. b
6. b	13. c	20. d	27. d	34. d
7. c	14. b	21. c	28. c	35. d

CHAPTER 17: ACRYLIC (METHACRYLATE) NAIL ENHANCEMENTS

1. a	9. b	17. a	25. a	33. a
2. b	10. a	18. b	26. b	34. a
3. b	11. c	19. a	27. d	35. d
4. a	12. c	20. b	28. b	36. b
5. d	13. d	21. b	29. c	37. b
6. c	14. a	22. d	30. c	
7. b	15. d	23. b	31. c	
8. a	16. d	24. a	32. a	

CHAPTER 18: UV GELS

1. d	6. a	11. b	16. c	21. a
2. b	7. b	12. c	17. d	22. d
3. d	8. c	13. d	18. a	23. d
4. b	9. a	14. d	19. a	24. d
5. d	10. d	15. d	20. a	25. b

CHAPTER 19: THE CREATIVE TOUCH

1. d	8. d	15. b	22. d	29. a
2. a	9. b	16. c	23. b	30. d
3. b	10. d	17. c	24. b	31. a
4. c	11. c	18. b	25. c	32. b
5. c	12. a	19. b	26. b	33. a
6. b	13. b	20. a	27. b	34. c
7. a	14. a	21. b	28. d	35. d

CHAPTER 20: SEEKING EMPLOYMENT

1. d	5. b	9. c	13. a	17. a
2. b	6. a	10. a	14. d	18. d
3. c	7. b	11. b	15. d	19. b
4. b	8. d	12. d	16. b	20. a

CHAPTER 21: ON THE JOB

1. c	6. a	11. c	16. d	21. a
2. c	7. c	12. b	17. b	22. d
3. d	8. c	13. a	18. b	23. b
4. c	9. d	14. b	19. a	24. b
5. a	10. a	15. a	20. a	25. d

CHAPTER 22: THE SALON BUSINESS

1. c	5. d	9. b	13. d	17. c
2. d	6. a	10. b	14. d	18. a
3. d	7. a	11. d	15. a	19. a
4. d	8. d	12. a	16. d	20. b

NOTES

NOTES

NOTES

NOTES

NOTES

NOTES

NOTES

NOTES